Elise
AT VICKSBURG

by
Jane H. Walker

PUBLISHED by PARABLES
Earthly Stories with a Heavenly Meaning

Elise At Vicksburg
Jane H. Walker

Published By
Parables
November, 2020

All Rights Reserved. No part of this book may be reproduced or utilized in any form or by any means, electronic or mechanical, including photocopying, recording, or by any information storage and retrieval system, without permission in writing from the author.

    ISBN 978-1-951497-98-9
    Printed in the United States of America

Readers should be aware that Internet Web sites offered as citations and/or sources for further information may have been changed or disappeared between the time this was written and the time it is read.

Elise
AT VICKSBURG

by
Jane H. Walker

PUBLISHED by PARABLES
Earthly Stories with a Heavenly Meaning

Other books by Jane H. Walker

Widow of Sighing Pines
2002
Recipient of the President's Award for Best Adult Fiction in 2003 Florida Publishers Association, Inc.

The Dodge Land Troubles, 1868-1923
2004
Coauthored with Chris Trowell, Professor Emeritus of South Georgia College, Douglas, Georgia

In the Lion's Paw
2008

Telfair County Images of America
2015
Coauthored with Robert Herndon

Can We Fathom the Nature of God?
(and America's Exceptionalism)
2018

Contact Information

Jane H. Walker can be reached through her website or by phone .
Website: widowofsighingpines.biz
Telephone number: 229-868-2243
P.O. Box #55357
Email: janewriter51@yahoo.com

DEDICATION

to

Brice and Dylan

and

to the belief that "all men are created equal"
and the hope "to form a more perfect Union"

ACKNOWLEDGMENTS

I extend great appreciation to Morgan Gates whose roots run deep in the fertile soil of Mississippi. His ancestors were among the first settlers of the Mississippi Territory and his great-great grandfather served in the Confederate Army defending Vicksburg in 1863. Earning a master's degree in both history and education from Historic Mississippi College, he served 28 years as an educator in the Vicksburg-Warren School District, teaching history and as an administrator before retiring. Morgan is currently serving as a licensed Battlefield Guide at the Vicksburg National Park.

Chris Trowell is an Associate Professor Emeritus from South Georgia College in Douglas, Georgia. He grew up in Oliver, Georgia, served in the U. S. Army, and is an alumnus of Georgia Southern University. Before his retirement in 1992, he taught history, geography and anthropology at South Georgia College. He served in several official capacities in the Society for Georgia Archaeology for twenty years. He served for several years on the Georgia National Register of Historic Places Review Board and the Douglas Historic Commission. He has assisted many authors and television producers who were researching articles, books, and videotapes on the Okefenokee Swamp and South Georgia history and archaeology. He has been a member of the board of directors of the Okefenokee Wildlife League for over a decade. He began studying the archaeology of the Ocmulgee Big Bend region and in 1981, he cooperated with the RAFT Project, a folklife program to reconstruct life along the Ocmulgee-Altamaha River during the logging-timber rafting era. Mr. Trowell has been a valuable resource for several of the books I have written. He is truly an historian extraordinaire.

I owe a debt of appreciation to the authors of journals and diaries which were kept during the Vicksburg Campaign by people on both sides of the conflict. Also, I derived much information from many of the books about the Battle of Vicksburg. Many of the events in the novel actually occurred and were gleaned from my reading of these writings.

I am indebted to my granddaughter, Brice, and her husband, Dylan Nelms, for their professional assistance in formatting the book.

FOREWORD

According to Confederate President, Jefferson Finis Davis, Vicksburg, Mississippi, was "the Gibraltar of America." Situated on bluffs rising hundreds of feet above the Mississippi River, Vicksburg was considered impregnable by friend and foe alike. President Abraham Lincoln believed its capture was the "key" to Union victory and that America would remain divided "until that key is in our pocket."

The campaign for Vicksburg began in April of 1862 when New Orleans, the South's largest city, was captured by Union forces, led by Commander David G. Farragut who next set his sights on Vicksburg. On June 28, 1862, Commander Farragut and Rear Admiral David D. Porter attempted a naval attack on the town, which ended in failure. For the next nine months, the Union army was defeated in five separate skirmishes to capture Vicksburg. In September of 1862, Confederates in Vicksburg began building a line of fortifications to protect their town from attacks from the East.

Needing to bypass the dangerous Confederate river batteries, Union General Ulysses S. Grant pressed into service many black laborers to dig canals which would allow his navy to position itself for the firing of artillery and the safety of its fleet. Two canals were begun north of Vicksburg, but one canal was dug through the De Soto Peninsula across the river from Vicksburg. It was later called Grant's Canal and was to be 1½ miles long. Though Grant hoped to divert the water of the Mississippi River to safer channels, away from the Rebel river batteries, the canals proved to be not only backbreaking work for the laborers but also, in the end, failures.

On December 29, 1862, General William Tecumsuh Sherman assaulted the Confederates at Chickasaw Bayou, five miles northeast of Vicksburg. This, along with other bayou expeditions, such as the Steele Bayou expedition, failed. When attempting to cross the almost impassable bayous north of Vicksburg, hip-deep in water, Union soldiers carried burning candles to light up the swamp for them to see. They also built corduroy roads and bridges to move men and supplies across the swamp. In late January of 1863, General Grant assembled federal forces in camps across from Vicksburg at Young's Point, Milliken's Bend, and Lake Providence in northeastern Louisiana, which numbered at that time around 45,000 men. Naval operations under Acting Rear Admiral David Porter, which would assist the Union land army, consisted of more than sixty boats, including ironclads, timberclads, tinclads, and auxiliary craft with more than three hundred guns and carrying 5,500 men. However, after so many failures, attempting to attack Vicksburg by water, General Grant finally decided that only a powerful land force could capture Vicksburg.

On January 1, 1863, President Lincoln issued his Emancipation Proclamation which gave all slaves freedom. President Lincoln stated that the Emancipation Proclamation was the most important aspect of his legacy. He said, "I never, in my life, felt more certain that I was doing right, than I do in signing this paper. If my name ever goes into history, it will be for this act, and my whole soul is in it."

General John C. Pemberton, a West Point graduate who knew Grant (also a West Point graduate), having fought with him in the Mexican War, was in command of the Confederate troops, defending the Mississippi River and the city of Vicksburg. Grant's fighting army swelled to 71,000 men, over double the size of Pemberton's army. From the outset of the Vicksburg campaign, General Pemberton corresponded with General Joseph Eggleston Johnston, believing that Johnston was coming with thousands of troop reinforcements, but these never materialized.

On April 16, 1863, on a starry but moonless night, General Grant was ready for his warships to "run" the Mississippi River past the dangerous Confederate batteries along the banks of Vicksburg. His plan was to use his ships to ferry thousands of his troops from the Louisiana side of the river to Bruinsburg on the eastern shore of the river, a number of miles below the city of Vicksburg. Seven armored gunboats with seventy-nine mounted guns and three armored transports laden with commissary stores, instead of troops, and a steam ram floated silently in single file down the dark river. Furnaces were banked to hide any smoke and all ports were covered and deck lights doused, except for deftly hooded lanterns visible only to the navigators for guidance. Coal-loaded barges were tied to the starboard sides of the warships, while river-soaked bales of hay were stacked around unprotected parts of the transports. Pets and poultry were put ashore to assure complete silence on-board.

General Grant, smoking a cigar, and his wife Julia were on the upper deck of one of the vessels, along with their twelve-year- old son, Fred. Their ten-year-old son, Ulysses, Junior, sat nearby on the knees of one of the Union officers. An Illinois private later described Grant whom he "saw standing on the upper deck of his headquarters boat a man of iron, his wife by his side. He seemed to me the most unmovable figure I ever saw."

The Confederate pickets who nightly patrolled the river in small boats soon discovered the silent fleet bearing down on them. As tar barrels along the bank were ignited, the pickets crossed the river and burned several houses in the village of De Soto, on the peninsula by that name directly across the river from Vicksburg, to illuminate the river further. They, of course, ran great risks of being captured by Federal forces on the opposite shore and also being exposed in the bright light of the burning houses to Union sharpshooters. Yet, they neither hesitated nor failed. To light up the river even more, the Rebels set fire to bales of cotton soaked in turpentine. However, enough Union boats made it through the Rebel blockade, followed by four more boats, towing large barges, two nights later, to ferry a large army across the river. As General Grant, holding his wife's hand, watched the fire power from both armies rain down upon each other, he later described it as "magnificent but terrible."

On April 30, 1863, President Abraham Lincoln issued a Proclamation for a National Day of Prayer and Fasting. The Proclamation began: "Whereas, the Senate of the United States, devoutly recognizing the Supreme Authority and just Government of Almighty God, in all the affairs of men and of nations, has, by a resolution, requested the President to designate and set apart a day for National prayer and humiliation." It continued: "And, insomuch as we know that, by His divine law, nations like individuals are subjected to punishments and chastisements in this world, may we not justly fear that the awful calamity of civil war, which now desolates the land, may be but a punishment, inflicted upon us, for our presumptuous sins, to the needful end of our national reformation as a whole people? We have been the recipients of the choicest bounties of Heaven. We have been preserved, these many years, in peace and prosperity. We have grown in numbers, wealth and power, as no other nation has ever grown. But we have forgotten God. We have forgotten the gracious hand which preserved us in peace, and multiplied and enriched and strengthened us; and we have vainly imagined, in the deceitfulness of our hearts, that all these blessings were produced by some superior wisdom and virtue of our own. Intoxicated with unbroken success, we have become too self-sufficient to feel the necessity of redeeming and preserving grace, too proud to pray to the God that made us! It behooves us then, to humble ourselves before the offended Power, to confess our national sins, and to pray for clemency and forgiveness."

Also, on April 30 and again on May 1, General Grant transported around 24,000 men and sixty field guns across the river to Bruinsburg Landing on the eastern shore of the river, a village thirty-five miles south of Vicksburg. Upon accomplishing this astounding feat, Grant later stated in his *Memoirs*: "When this was effected I felt a degree of relief scarcely ever equaled since. Vicksburg was not yet taken it is true, nor were its defenders demoralized by any of our previous moves. I was now in the enemy's country, with a vast river and the stronghold of Vicksburg between me and my base of supplies. But I was on dry ground on the same side of the river with the enemy. All the campaigns, labors, hardships and exposures from the month of December previous to this time that had been made and endured, were for the accomplishment of this one object." Ironically, it was an ex-slave who told Grant that there were no Confederate soldiers at Bruinsburg.

On May 1, seven thousand men left the Rebel trenches along the river at Grand Gulf and marched south to Port Gibson to do battle with the northern troops of General Grant, which were now on the eastern shore of the Mississippi River. Grant pushed his men up the banks to take possession of the bridge over the bayou, but was surprised by Confederates waiting on the nearby hilltop. The attack began at midnight with the Federals steadily pushing the Rebels back, confident that they would soon accomplish their goal. The two armies faced each other on two hills with a valley below, through which meandered a small stream. Over this water hung a few stunted trees and thick bushes.

Several other Federal brigades, including Sherman's corps which arrived on May 8th, transported thousands of men across the river to Grand Gulf, bringing the total federal force on the eastern side of the Mississippi River to about 45,000 men at that time. Grant's army waited below the mouth of Bayou Pierre, a deep and muddy stream with impassible banks and partly filled by backwater. The bridge near the entrance to the town of Port Gibson was the only means of passage over the bayou.

In the morning the federal brigade had flags fluttering in defiance as sunshine glistened on their gun barrels and bayonets. Iron hail rained down on both armies as they met at the stream below them. Bullets flew so fast and the noise was so incessant that one of the Union brigades became confused and occupied open ground, allowing the Rebels to decimate them until they broke for shelter. Few leaves or twigs were left on the bare poles which survived the onslaught. Little did the Rebels know that the large federal army extended nearly a mile on their left and was rapidly closing around them. According to Kevin Dougherty, author of *The Vicksburg Campaign*, Grant spared Port Gibson because he found the town "too beautiful to burn." However, the Union soldiers ransacked the town, taking books from the library to use as toilet paper. When a hard-riding courier reached the Confederates with the desperate order to retreat, it was enough to make the toughest soldier cry.

On May 12, while en route to the capital city of Jackson, the Union Army also captured the town of Raymond. According to Anne Martin, daughter of the *Vicksburg Whig* editor, Marmaduke Shannon, "that immense army pour[ed] into [Raymond], flaunting their star-spangled banner, playing Yankee Doodle, and, oh, the desecration! The Bonnie Blue Flag…All night the fife and drum was heard as fresh regiments passed…we could hear them tearing down fences, shooting cattle, shouting and going on and we expected every minute to be broke in on…the doors were locked but they broke them open and took everything but one sidesaddle, even pulled the curtains down and tore them in strings. The remaining sidesaddle was taken by one of these fancy yellow [mulatto] girls, an especial pet of one of their officers…We could see them bringing all kinds of plunder, showing around silverware and jewelry they had stolen. If you are ever invaded, Emmie, don't bury anything…Hearing that Mrs. Robinson had buried her silverware, they dug up every foot of her garden until they found it. Mrs. Durden's baby was buried in the yard and would you believe it: that child's remains were dug [up] no less than three different times in search of treasure. This is how we fared at the hands of the Yankees."

As if to corroborate the above mistreatment of the southerners during the war, General William Tecumseh Sherman felt that the South must be subjugated and made to comprehend that "we will remove & destroy every obstacle, if need be take every life, every acre of land, every particle of property, everything that to us seems proper, and we will not cease till the end is attained, that all who do not aid [us] are enemies, and we will not account to them for our acts. If the People of the South oppose [us] they do at their own peril, and if they stand by, mere lookers on the domestic tragedy, they have no right to immunity, protection or share in the final Result….I would not coax [the South] or even meet them half way, but make them so sick & tired of war that Generations would pass before they would ever again appeal to it."

According to Colonel S.H. Lockett, C.S.A., Chief Engineer of the Defenses, he stated in his *The Defense of Vicksburg* that the Federals were sending signals to each other from a tall tower on land to a masthead on Admiral Porter's ship. He also stated that the Confederates had learned the Federal Code on the ciphering principle of Edgar Allan Poe's short story, "The Gold Bug." Poe was popularly regarded as a ciphering expert.

To protect themselves from the Union missiles hurled at the

city from the West, the citizens of Vicksburg began digging caves to live in during the battle. The caves faced the East and were not as safe, once the Federal Army encircled the city from the East. However, they proved to keep the injuries and deaths of the city's populace to a minimum during the horrific conflict, for less than twenty civilians were killed during the 47-day siege. More died from the effects of malnutrition and infection and disease than from the enemy's actions. This held true for the soldiers who defended Vicksburg, also.

On May 14, the Federals captured the capital city of Jackson. In Grant's *Personal Memoirs*, he wrote: "I slept that night in the room that Johnston had occupied the night before." He also wrote in regard to the capture of Jackson the following observance: "About four in the afternoon I sent for the corps commanders and directed the dispositions to be made of their troops. Sherman was to remain in Jackson until he destroyed that place as a railroad center, and manufacturing city of military supplies. He did the work most effectually. Sherman and I went together into a manufactory which had not ceased work on account of the battle nor for the entrance of Yankee troops. Our presence did not seem to attract the attention of either the manager or the operatives, most of whom were girls. We looked on for a while to see the tent cloth which they were making roll out of the looms, with "C.S.A." woven in each bolt. There was an immense amount of cotton, in bales, stacked outside. Finally, I told Sherman I thought they had done work enough. The operatives were told they could leave and take with them what cloth they could carry. In a few minutes cotton and factory were in a blaze."

The city of Jackson endured being captured and recaptured five times by Federal troops during the war. During its first occupation, "the revelry was such that one-thousand-dollar Confederate bills were mockingly used to light pipes," according to *The Vicksburg Campaign* by Kevin Dougherty. While the Federals were engaged with the capture of Jackson, Confederates continued their work, begun in September of 1862, building more fortifications of redoubts, redans, and lunettes which circled the eastern side of Vicksburg in a jagged, roughly seven to nine-mile crescent.

The battle of Champion Hill, or Baker's Creek as it is sometimes called, was the bloodiest fought of the Vicksburg campaign. Champion Hill was the cotton plantation of Sid and Matilda Champion. Its canebrake-infested slopes of some seventy feet downward brought about a comment from an Indiana soldier that his company had to "pull ourselves up the sides of the ravines by the bushes." It was captured by the Union on May 16 after returning victoriously from Jackson. The Northern troops numbered 32,000; Confederates numbered 23,000. Pemberton had 3,840 casualties, while Grant listed his as 2,457. The battle for Champion Hill was called by Union General James B. McPherson "one of the most murderous of the war." Union General Alvin Hovey called it "the hill of death."

Since Champion Hill was General Pemberton's first field battle, and he did not perform well, a Confederate surgeon named John A. Leavy wrote the following words in his diary on May 16th:

> "Today proved to the army and the country the value of a general. Pemberton is either a traitor, or the most incompetent officer in the Confederacy. *Indecision, Indecision, Indecision*…is he a traitor? Time will show…We have been badly defeated where we might have given the enemy a severe repulse. We have been defeated in detail and have lost. O God! How many brave and gallant soldiers."

William F. Crummer of the 45th Illinois, Smith's brigade, described what the field at Champion Hill looked like, once the firing stopped:

> "I would like to portray the scene that we gazed upon. It was a horrible picture and one that I carry with me to this day. All around us lay the dead and dying, amid the groans and cries of the wounded. Our surgeons came up quickly and, taking possession of a farm house, converted it into a hospital, and we began to carry ours and the enemy's wounded to the surgeons. There they lay, the blue and the gray intermingled; the same rich, young American blood flowing out in little rivulets of crimson; each thinking he was in the right; the one conscious of it today, the other admitting now it were best the Union should be maintained one and inseparable.
>
> "The surgeons made no preference as to which should be the first treated; the blue and the gray took their turn before the surgeon's knife. What heroes some of those fellows were, with no anesthetic to sooth the agony, but gritting their teeth, they bore the pain of the knife and saw, while arms and legs were being severed from their bodies." According to Timothy B. Smith's *Champion Hill, Decisive Battle for Vicksburg*, General Grant ordered his surgeons to 'be sure to treat the Confederate wounded just as if they were our own wounded.'"

After the war, a Union physician told a Champion descendant that "while performing amputations on her dining room table, the blood would get so deep on the floor that a soldier had to take an ax and cut a hole in the floor so the blood could run out under the house."

Lastly, before the final siege of the city, Grant's engineers began building bridges across the Big Black River, by torchlight during the night, to facilitate the crossing of their troops over the swamp. Their building materials consisted of cotton bales, trees, and wood from nearby buildings.

On May 18, when the 47-day siege of the city of Vicksburg began, it was announced that enough provisions had been stored away to feed the Confederate army for six months. In less than one month, however, the food reduction and its inedible quality were apparent. Short rations of corn bread and poor quality of beef became the norm. Finally, the only bread obtainable was made from cowpeas which were usually cultivated in the South as provender for animals. The peas were ground into meal at a large mill in the city, then sent to the cooks in the camp to be prepared. The meal was mixed with cold water and baked, but it never got done, no matter how long it cooked. The longer it baked, the harder on the outside it became, but the inside remained raw. The result was the hardest of "hard tack," Captain E. E. Houston, of General J. C. Vaughn's Confederate staff, stated. He said that the bread on the outside "was so hard that one might have knocked down a full-grown steer with a chunk of it." During the last weeks of the siege, the people of Vicksburg were reduced to eating mules, dogs, cats, rats and even shoe leather.

Though the Federals were for a time directly across from the town of Vicksburg, as black ex-slaves and others worked on the doomed canal, they were next observed around the middle of May on the De Soto Peninsula. According to Sergeant William Tunnard, C.S.A., author of "A Southern Record: The History of the Third Regiment Louisiana Infantry," written in 1866, "On the peninsula the white tents of the enemy's encampment were plainly visible."

In the early morning hours of May 22, the Federals had ringed the east of Vicksburg with their own fortifications which stretched for nearly 15½ miles, from Haynes Bluff, north of Vicksburg, to Warrenton, south of Vicksburg, and launched an attack against the Confederate stockade until midmorning, tearing off large splinters on the parapet. Around fifty men, carrying scaling ladders, ran to the ditch where they planted their colors on the outer edge of the Confederate parapet.

Baldwin's Ferry Road was the only place where the Yankees succeeded in making a breakthrough. However, General Waul's Texas legion men in gray dashed up the hill and with bayonets fixed, actually pushed the Federals over the parapet into the trench. There, they were shot as they ran.

In late spring of 1863, the town of Milliken's Bend, Louisiana, about twelve miles northwest of Vicksburg, was occupied by 1250 ex-slaves who had fled from the surrounding plantations and their former masters and by only 160 whites. General Grant had set up camp at Milliken's Bend for the defecting slaves, known as contrabands. This was a site of supply depots and hospitals, many of which were operated and guarded by United States Colored Troops, some of whom were recently recruited freedmen. The Battle of Milliken's Bend was likely the best example of courageous black men during the Civil War.

Historian Martha M. Bigelow of Mississippi College penned in her 1960 article in the *Journal of Negro History* that the blacks "were to perform a service to their race and to write the name of Milliken's Bend into history." Assistant Secretary of War, Charles A. Dana, observed that "the bravery of the Blacks at Milliken's Bend completely revolutionized the sentiment of the Army with regard to the employment of Negro troops." One black regiment had only been given their rifles the day before the battle. Black historian Benjamin Quarles stated that "one Negro took his former master a prisoner and brought him into camp with great gusto."

On the thirty-first day of the siege, around June 17, the city of Vicksburg was bombed with huge iron spheres weighing almost three hundred pounds. Filled with gunpowder, they flew through the air with burning fuses which left a path of smoke by day and fire by night. According to a chronicle kept by Willie Lord, son of the Reverend W.W. Lord, rector of Christ Episcopal Church, "A peculiar hissing, screaming noise accompanied their flight and, exploding with tremendous violence, they wrecked houses and streets like small earthquakes."

Christ Episcopal Church and the Roman Catholic Church were the only churches where services were held throughout the siege. Daily, the Reverend W.W. Lord, rector of Christ Church and dressed in priestly attire, opened the church, rang the bell and stood behind the chancel rail, awaiting his flock which grew smaller as the siege intensified.

According to Winston Groom, author of *Vicksburg 1863*, the Confederates did everything possible to defend Vicksburg, including mounting the huge 10-inch columbiads on a railcar and running it up and down the tracks at Port Hudson, firing on different Yankee positions. Though this is disputed by some as myth, Groom, nevertheless, included it in his book. The Yankees called the formidable weapon the "Demoralizer," because of its unearthly noise and because of the deadly "missiles" which issued from it. Because the Rebels were short on regular cannon shot, they rammed anything they could find down the barrels of the guns, including "flatirons, ball-bearings, nails, railroad spikes, nuts and bolts, hatchet-heads, rocks, sugarcane knives," and, also, "broken pieces of bayonets."

Elise At Vicksburg

When Captain J. J. Kellogg of Company B., of 113th Illinois Infantry, and his regiment were moved to the mouth of the Yazoo River, he wrote:

> "At first the blue waters of the Yazoo fooled us. It was as blue and clear as lake water and we drank copiously of it, but felt badly afterwards. We didn't know we were drinking poisoned water until an old colored citizen one day warned us. Then we looked the matter up and found that the interpretation of the word 'Yazoo' was 'the river of death' and that its beautiful blue waters were the drainings of vast swamps and swales."

The Yazoo was also home to alligators, and at least one Union soldier had his arm badly mangled by an alligator when he went swimming in the Yazoo. As he was near death, two of his buddies managed to fight off the reptile and save his life. Confederate couriers who brought messages from the outside world had to swim in the river, thereby risking their lives because of the alligators and illnesses brought on by the fetid waters of the swamp.

Captain Thomas H. Parker, with the 51 Regiment of Pennsylvania Volunteers, was encamped on Snyder's Bluff nine miles above Vicksburg. Being aware of health dangers in regard to the swamps, he posted the following sanitary orders:

> "…to all the regiments for cautionary measures against that scourge of all sickness: the yellow fever. It warns us not to expose ourselves unnecessarily to the scorching rays of the sun in daytime or to the damp and chilly night air; also

to use no water for drinking or culinary purposes other than that obtained from wells and springs, in which barrels or boxes must be sunk for the purpose of guarding them against any uncleanly matter finding its way into the water, which undoubtedly would be the case in the event of rain, for the current of water which necessarily must flow down the deep gullies and ravines would wash or carry down in its rushing career the carcasses of dead mules and other filth that accumulates from one rain 'till another. We are recommended to bathe our persons at least twice a week…this is the greatest country that we have been in yet for insects of all descriptions. Here is where you can find your fine, plump mosquitoes, sandflies, beetles, bugs, ants, worms of all kinds, ticks and in fact anything in the insect line."

Then, in a race against time, both the Confederates and the Union Army began digging trenches and mines which zigzagged toward each other. These proved to provide the last battle for the capture of Vicksburg. At times, both could hear the spades and picks and the voices of the enemy as they dug. Sometimes, they would holler out to each other and even exchange certain products, such as tobacco for coffee, which they would toss to one another. Sometimes, a soldier would throw a grenade into the enemy's trench, only to have it caught and returned to the sender.

At night, on June 24, the Union Army had dug forty feet under the 3rd Louisiana Redan, referred to as Fort Hill. Into this mine, their sappers deposited 2,200 pounds of explosive. The different powder chambers were sealed with sandbags, cross-timbers and other materials to exacerbate the force of the explosion.

On June 25, in midafternoon, the mine was detonated, creating a crater twenty feet deep and fifty feet in diameter, according to Colonel S.H. Lockett, C.S.A., Chief Engineer of the Defenses. A soldier in the 3rd Louisiana Redan stated, "Suddenly the earth under our feet gave a convulsive shudder and with a muffled roar a mighty column of earth, men, wagons, poles, spades and guns rose many feet in the air. About fifty lives were blotted out in that instant." The Union Army surged into the opening created but were deterred when the Rebels wheeled an artillery piece into place and began firing, killing the Union marksmen at close range. The crater was referred to as "the death hole" and the "slaughter pit."

As the siege continued, the enemy redoubled their efforts to reduce the city to rubble, if need be. After reveille in the dark, early morning hours, the northern army maintained ceaseless fire. Strong and secure fortifications appeared. Military federal redoubts manned by expert sharpshooters were on the front lines. Blazing with artillery, parapets were erected on every knoll and workable elevation of the landscape. The Confederate dead were buried in trenches fifty feet long and three feet wide—six bodies to a trench. Then, as a mourner observed, they were "lowered into the cold earth which was hastily heaped above the mortal remains." Of course, Union and Rebel dead were often buried where they died and, also, near field hospitals where they died.

The Union Navy continued its bombardment of the city from beyond the peninsula on the western side of the city, its mortars presenting pyrotechnics as luminous and bright as twinkling stars. Traversing the sky in rising parabolas, they exploded with vicious shrieks, scattering their lethal fragments over the besieged city. Ejected from four miles away, at forty-five- degree angles, the fuses followed the iron monsters like large

October meteors whose dazzling brilliancy was subdued by the terrifying whirr of jagged iron, bent on death and destruction. The weight of these missiles varied from a hundred twenty-eight to two hundred and forty pounds.

Finally, the superior strength of the Northern military which outnumbered the Confederates more than two to one, prevailed, and white flags appeared on the top ridges of the ravines which had been guarded by the Confederates. From March 29, 1863-July 4, 1863, the full campaign claimed 10,142 Union casualties and 9,091 Confederate casualties, including both killed and injured. Colonel Lockett stated that "General Grant says there was no cheering by the Federal troops. My recollection is that on our right a hearty cheer was given by one Federal division 'for the gallant defenders of Vicksburg!'" The battle for the city of Vicksburg was over. Now, the "key" to the survival of the United States was proverbially in the pocket of President Abraham Lincoln, and the great Mississippi River flowed unvexed to the sea.

However, General Grant did write in his *Personal Memoirs* that "The small arms of the enemy were far superior to the bulk of ours. Up to this time our troops at the West had been limited to the old United States flint-lock muskets changed into percussion, or the Belgian musket imported early in the war—almost as dangerous to the person firing it as to the one aimed at—and a few new and improved arms. These were of many different calibers, a fact that caused much trouble in distributing ammunition during an engagement. The enemy had generally new arms which had run he blockade and were of uniform caliber. After the surrender I authorized all colonels whose regiments were armed with inferior muskets, to place them in the stack of captured arms and replace them with the latter."

Below is General Ulysses Grant's missive to General

Pemberton in regard to terms of surrender:

"Headquarters Department of Tennessee,
Before Vicksburg, July 4, 1863
Lieutenant General Pemberton, commanding forces in Vicksburg:

General: I have the honor to acknowledge your communication of the 3d of July. The amendments proposed by you cannot be acceded to in full. It will be necessary to furnish every officer and man with a parole signed by myself, which, with the completion of the rolls of prisoners, will necessarily take some time. Again: I can make no stipulation with regard to the treatment of citizens and their private property. While I do not propose to cause any of them any undue annoyance or loss, I cannot consent to leave myself under restraint by stipulations. The property which officers can be allowed to take with them will be as stated in the proposition of last evening—that is, that officers will be allowed their private baggage and side arms, and mounted officers one horse each. If you mean by your propositions for each brigade to march to the front of the lines now occupied by it, and stack their arms at ten o'clock, A.M., and then return to the inside and remain as prisoners until properly paroled, I will make no objections to it. Should no modification be made of your acceptance of my terms by nine o'clock, A.M., I shall regard them as having been rejected, and act accordingly. Should these terms be accepted, white flags will be displayed along your lines to prevent such of my troops as may not have been notified from firing on your men.

I am, General, very respectfully, your obedient servant,
U.S. GRANT, MAJOR GENERAL UNITED STATES ARMY."

On July 13, 1863, the long-suffering but then ecstatic President

Lincoln wrote the following letter to General Grant:

> "I do not remember that you and I ever met personally. I write this now as a grateful acknowledgment for the almost inestimable service you have done the country. I wish to say a word further. When you first reached the vicinity of Vicksburg, I thought you should do, what you finally did—march the troops across the neck, run the batteries with the transports, and thus go below; and I never had any faith, except a general hope that you knew better than I, that the Yazoo Pass expedition, and the like, could succeed. When you got below and took Port Gibson, Grand Gulf, and vicinity, I thought you should go down the river and join Gen. Banks; and when you turned Northward East of the Big Black, I feared it was a mistake. I now wish to make the personal acknowledgment that you were right, and I was wrong.
> Yours very truly,
> Abraham Lincoln"

The city of Vicksburg did not celebrate Independence Day for 81 years, since its surrender occurred on the same day of the month, July 4, 1863. However, after the end of World War II, Vicksburg joined the rest of the nation in celebrating Independence Day. Added to the patriotic fervor after the war was a visit by General Dwight D. Eisenhower, which set the stage for a return to celebrating the birth of our nation.

Elise At Vicksburg

Chapter One
April, 1863

The train at Jackson was taking on wood for the trip to Vicksburg, as the Holmes family said their goodbyes to one another. Gripping his crutches, Wade Holmes first kissed his wife, Abby, then turned with some difficulty to kiss his two children who would be going with her to Vicksburg. Eighteen-year-old Elise reached up and kissed her father's bearded cheek, being careful not to cause him to lose his balance. Young Jack Holmes, at the age of fourteen, being taller than his sister and almost as tall as his father, threw his arms around his father, nearly making him lose his grip on the crutches. "Now hear me, Jack," Wade Holmes said, his eyes welling with tears, "I want you to look after your mother and sister. God willing, the younger boys and I will be following you to Vicksburg in a few days. I don't want to hear any more about your joining the Rebs there, you hear?"

"But, Papa," Jack said, "boys are joining younger than me. Why, I heard just yesterday that boys way younger than me are fighting for the Cause. Please give me your permission, Papa," he said with a beseeching look at his father.

The two younger boys looked from their father's anguished face to their brother's eager one, hopeful that their father would indeed give their older brother permission to join the fight. Mark, age ten, and Jeremy, age eight, waited breathlessly for his answer.

"Look at my leg, Jack, or what's left of it. You know that the rest of it was left on the battlefield at Shiloh." Though they had seen their father's battle wound many times, their eyes were drawn to the pants leg that dangled below what was once a leg and foot.

"Our men are winning the war, Jack. They don't need a youngster to help them. We'll stay awhile in Vicksburg, where we'll all be safe. The Yanks have been trying for a year or more to capture the city, with no success. I'm told that Grant, himself, is there across the river on the Louisiana side." Jack dropped his head as he listened to his father's reply, then reached down to hug his two young brothers.

Elise and her mother gave the two younger boys quick hugs and kisses before entering the train, with Jack following behind them. Upon entering the wooden train car, they realized it was nearly filled with soldiers, apparently on their way to join the war at Vicksburg. Attired in the gray uniform of the Confederacy, all of the young men stood and waited until Elise and her mother and brother were seated, before sitting down again. Looking out the train window, Elise for the first time noticed the mounting chaos outside the depot, with baggage being thrown hurriedly and carelessly into the baggage car of the train. People elbowed one another as they sought the Mobile and Vicksburg cars. Horses were rearing up with fright, and Negroes seemed confused about where to go. She saw what appeared to be a runaway slave who was chained and dragged along by an angry-looking white man.

Elise noticed her father hopping toward his carriage with his younger sons romping ahead of him. Cuffey, their wiry Negro servant, helped Wade Holmes into the carriage, then reached down and hoisted his sons up beside him. After closing the door, he pulled himself up to the driver's seat. As the train began a slow chug from the station, Elise and her mother and brother waved, being rewarded by waves from inside the carriage and, also, from Cuffey who let go of the reins with one hand and waved farewell to the clanking train.

Several days before, Elise had overheard her father and mother talking about the Vicksburg trip. It was agreed that her father and her younger brothers would make the trip later, after the family silver and china were hidden and the remaining livestock sold. There was the question of whether it was best to bury the silver somewhere on their property, which would leave telltale dirt displacement, or whether to lower it into the well. Also, there was no one they could trust to hide their family keepsakes, as her father was not able to do it. They dared not ask Cuffey to help them, as they had talked to too many of their friends and relatives who had entrusted their servants with their prized property, only to have them abscond with the same or tell the Yankees where such could be found. Wade Holmes knew it was just a matter of time, and a short while at that, before Cuffey and their other servants fled to the North's side. He felt fortunate that their servants were still with them, but he knew it wouldn't be for long.

Some of their silver was old, from generations before, with different family initials and crests on some of the flatware and serving pieces. Elise had always enjoyed seeing the silver pieces used when her parents had guests to eat. These were times before her mother's health became so fragile. She never did hear what exactly was the plan to hide the silver. The Yanks had become downright cunning in finding where the Southerners were hiding their valuables.

Elise remembered hearing her cousin talking about Burnside's army during the battle at Fredericksburg, Virginia, where she lived. They broke open locked doors and took everything they could get their hands on. All night, the fife and drum were heard as fresh regiments in the massive army passed through the town. Flaunting their star-spangled banner, with

"Yankee Doodle" filling the air, they tore down fences, shot cattle, and dug up every foot of a lady's garden, finally finding her silverware. Elise remembered hearing about drunken Union soldiers plundering houses, ruining oil paintings, and frolicking around town in women's clothing. She shivered at the horror of it all. Her cousin said that General Robert E. Lee stated it was the most vicious and shameless looting he had seen during the war.

As the train rattled along the wooden crossties, Elise's thoughts turned to her family which was unusually close because sisters had married brothers. Her Uncle Alan Holmes was her father's brother, and her Aunt Celia Elise Holmes was her mother's sister, for whom she was named. She had always felt special because she shared her favorite aunt's name. Her first name was the same also. She, too, was Celia Elise Holmes.

The afternoon was rapidly turning to evening as the conductor appeared in the car, first gathering the tickets, then lighting the candles at both ends of the car, which were needed as darkness set in. The train gathered a little speed as the several filled coaches rumbled through the countryside. Many of the soldiers had found room on top of the train, once the coaches were filled, and their legs and boots dangled over the sides of the cars. With the windows up, the cooler air inside was refreshing, though it brought cinders from the smokestack and dust from the surrounding fields.

Elise was glad that she and her mother had worn linen dusters over their dresses for protection from the grime of rail travel. She glanced at her mother who sat by the window with her eyes closed. *She looks tired and frail,* Elise thought, before letting her gaze rest on the soldiers in the car. She felt conspicuous as one of only two women in the coach. Several of the men met her eyes as she looked around, causing her to look away and to glance at her mother again.

"I'm not asleep, Elise," Abby Holmes whispered, "but it'll be several hours before we reach Vicksburg. I brought your Aunt Celia's letter with me, if you want to read it."

"No, there isn't much light, Mama. What does she say?"

"Well, there's going to be a ball sometime soon. She and Alan will be going, and she wants us to go, too. She wants to take you to Madame Cognaisse's place for a Parisian-modeled gown for the ball."

"Oh, Mama, you mean they're still having frolics and balls?" Without thinking, she let out a little squeal that brought unwanted attention from some of the nearest soldiers.

"That's what she said in her letter. That's the reason we're all going to stay in Vicksburg until the war is over, dear. They're still able to live the way we used to, before the war began. Everyone says Vicksburg is a fortress and will never be taken. Also, Elise, the soldiers will be coming to the ball. You may meet an eligible young man from a good family."

Elise smiled and slightly rolled her eyes at her mother's last comment. The war had taken away many of the young men of Jackson and surrounding areas, and the social life of the town had been greatly diminished. Elise had missed the frolics and parties that always marked the debuts of young women into the society of adulthood. Vicksburg might bring back normalcy and gaiety into her young life. Her lips smiled and her eyes glistened at the thought.

She looked across the aisle at her young brother, sitting beside a soldier who couldn't be much older than her brother. He was, in fact, not as tall as her brother. The two were whispering, and Elise heard the word "bordello" mentioned several times. She had an idea what one was, and she knew it was nothing good. She made a mental note to ask her friend, Drusie, about it. Drusilla Davis had lived in Vicksburg all of her life. They had been best friends for several years and had exchanged letters, but there was so much to catch up about in person, and Elise looked forward to hearing Drusie's comments about the bordello in Vicksburg.

The train rumbled on slowly for several hours, its passengers either asleep or talking quietly to one another. Many of the soldiers stuck their legs out of the open windows, to give them more room and some fresh air. Abby Holmes slept, lulled by the rocking of the moving train. As the train neared Vicksburg, Elise could see camps and campfires with the silhouettes of men moving around them. She then saw the Confederate sentinel guarding the Black River Bridge, silent and erect. He maintained a salute as the train clickety-clacked over the bridge.

Farther along, she saw companies of soldiers on the road, marching quietly toward Vicksburg, the sound of their boots muffled by the passing train. Wagons of artillery next came into view. Many white-covered wagons passed through the ravines, driven by teamsters who cracked their whips, bringing to life the dark, silent night. She saw large excavations into the hills on the eastern side of the town and realized that these were the caves she had heard about. Some were lit by candles and lanterns, and she wondered whether people were already living in them.

The caves looked ominous and she couldn't imagine staying in one, or even entering one, for any length of time. Finally, the train reached the depot, crowded with soldiers waiting to leave. Elise wondered where they would be going, if they were not staying to defend the city.

As the train slowly groaned to a halt, its shrill whistle sounding and its bell clanging, she stared out the window, trying to find her aunt's fine landau carriage which would be pulled by the large Percherons named Beau and Roi. She had always smiled about the fact that her aunt had even given their horses French names. Once she saw the carriage, with its top rolled back, and the two horses near the baggage car, she roused her brother and her mother who both were asleep, and they left the coach. Still not fully awake, Abby and Jack stumbled behind Elise who waved her hand to Scipio, her aunt's colored servant. Old "Sip," as he was called, smiled in recognition and drove the carriage over to a nearby carriage block. As he let himself down, the baggage handler hurried over, motioning to Sip.

"Hello, Uncle," he said in a loud voice, "how long before you'll be moving the carriage?"

"Won't be long, Massuh." Satisfied with his answer, the baggage handler hurried off, yelling to others who were waiting with their carriages. Sip smiled and welcomed Abby to Vicksburg.

"Miz Sissy, she sho' nuff lookin' fo' you all. It late, but she say she stayin' up, waitin' fo you. An' Massuh Alan, too. How you doin', Miz Abby?" Elise had forgotten that almost everyone, including her brother, Jack, called her aunt "Sissy," except her mother who often called her aunt "Sister."

"I'm all right, Sip. I declare, it's good to see you," Abby said with a smile, as Sip assisted her entry into the open carriage. Grinning broadly, Sip turned to welcome the others.

"And Miz 'Lise and Massuh Jack," he said, "Lawd, how you chillun done growed! We ain' seen you since de war stahrted mebbe."

"You're right, Sip. It's been awhile since we've seen you," Elise said with a smile as the old servant helped her into the carriage.

As Jack jumped into the carriage, he said, "Well, you haven't changed at all, Sip!"

"Jest a mite slower," Scipio said, his grin showing several missing teeth. After closing the carriage door, he climbed back up to the driver's seat and clucked to the matched, gray geldings.

Though the carriage lanterns provided some light for the trip to the Holmes' plantation home, the many fires burning throughout the city lit up the town and the river below it. Lights also glowed from the warships up the river, reminding everyone in the carriage of the presence of the northern enemy fleet. Though the best stores and shops lined Washington Street, the jolting drive through the city on the clay thoroughfare, now pitted from missiles lobbed from Federal gunboats upriver, revealed closed businesses, their facades lit by tall gas lanterns. Along the riverbank, as Elise remembered, row after row of warehouses alternated with the rugged shacks of Irish laborers, now empty because of the war. Confederate entrenchments were dug in now, between the street and the river.

Soldiers meandered along the streets, some in full uniform, others in ragtag attire. Elise winced at how thin they looked. Seeing people hurrying here and there, Elise noticed a gentleman walking down the street with a fish in one hand and a cavalry saddle on his back. In his other hand, he carried a bridle and newspapers and blankets. He seemed oblivious of everyone else and of his surroundings. She wondered why no one seemed to think he looked odd. Maybe, she thought, it was because almost everyone seemed to have his own personal mission to accomplish. People were grappling with the conditions of war as best they could, and each had his own way of coming to terms with the disruptions of their lives.

Horses, belonging to the officers and tied to the trees near the tents of the river entrenchments, reared up on their hind legs and nibbled at cane tops and mulberry leaves of the few trees left intact from the steady cannonades up the river. Elise shuddered as she looked at the mules whose rib cages were obvious through their almost skeleton torsos. She wondered how they were strong enough to bear the burdens of war.

Farther away from the river, Greek Revival homes, shielded by fences and hedges, spoke volumes about the wealth of many in the town of Vicksburg. However, gates were swung open in front of these estates now, with cattle foraging among the flowers and gardens which were no longer tended with care. Less pretentious houses were built even farther away from the river, some of which required climbing several flights of steps to get to the front doors, because of the hilly lay of the land.

As the carriage rolled along the main street, Elise inhaled the residual miasma of odors which emanated from the coal smoke of the river steamers which once plied their trades on the Mississippi River below and the mules and tar and some of the dirty, muddy side streets of the war-torn town. However, as they neared her aunt's and uncle's home, a heavy redolence of early-blooming magnolias filled the air, and Elise remembered the fragrances of gardenias and jasmine which she had always associated with the town. Vicksburg was filled with blooming flowers almost every season of the year, including violets, morning-glories, roses, and chrysanthemums. Away from the shanties along the river, it was a city of great beauty, and it saddened her to see its devastation.

Upon entering the long cobblestone drive of her aunt's and uncle's lovely plantation house, Elise was glad that the place was much as she remembered, for she had spent many summers at her namesake's home. The large wrought-iron gate stayed open most of the time, as she remembered. The wrought-iron grillwork on the front of the large house had been brought by boat from New Orleans up the Mississippi River. It was among the finest of many lovely homes in Vicksburg. Being of French ancestry, her Aunt Celia loved anything that evoked that part of her lineage, and Elise did, also.

Inside the gate was the old wrought-iron marker with the

name Belle Voir fashioned in a way that only her aunt could have designed. Elise vaguely remembered it, but didn't appreciate its beauty then, as she did now. Soft light from several huge, gas-burning post lanterns framed the exterior of the large home which had more lacy grill work around the double front door and over the windows of the second floor. A fine horse was tethered in front of the house, as if waiting for its rider to appear. The front lights barely revealed the servants' quarters in the rear of the house and the separate kitchen.

Behind the house, she could see the beginnings of a rail fence that trailed off into the darkness and a few cows which stood in the soft light near the kitchen. She could barely make out the crops in the fields behind the house. Old Scipio halted the horses before the carriage block and climbed down before opening the door of the carriage and helping each one descend to the grand, circular driveway.

"Miz Abby, ifn' you gives me de baggage ticket, ah go back to de depot an git it fuh you."

Rummaging in her pocket, Abby produced the ticket. "Goodness gracious, Sip," she said with a smile, "I guess I forgot our baggage."

As the old servant left for the return trip to the train station, the front door of the palatial home opened wide and Alan and Celia Holmes welcomed their guests with outstretched arms.

"How was your trip? You were lucky to get here before the Yanks tear up the tracks," Alan Holmes said.

"The trip was fine," Abby said, as they all moved inside. Alan and Celia Holmes hugged each one, as Celia asked whether they needed anything to eat or drink.

"No, we don't need a thing, Sister. We had an early supper in Jackson. Sip has gone to get our baggage. We just appreciate your invitation to come to Vicksburg, where we'll be safe," Abby said.

Elise hugged her aunt again, telling her how beautiful Belle Voir was, that it was the same as she remembered. Jack, too, added his compliments about the house and grounds.

"Well," Celia said, "I must tell you that things aren't at all the same as they once were. Thank goodness we still have our two horses and our carriage, but they may be taken at any time. The soldiers have taken our other horses and most of our cattle, but we still have our mule. Our boys have to be fed, so they just take what they need. We only have three cows left. The crops are rotting in the fields. Our field hands are all gone…guess they made it across the river to the Yankee side. We are left without anyone to look after the crops. All of our servants, except Old Scipio and Chloee, have gone over to the Yankee side. Someone said they ride logs and rafts across the river to the Louisiana side."

For the first time since their decision to go to Vicksburg, Elise had a feeling of apprehension. Maybe things were not the best in Vicksburg, after all. As if reading Elise's thoughts, her aunt began reassuring the three of them.

"Listen, dear ones, we will all be fine. General Pemberton and our soldiers say that Vicksburg will never be taken. Alan says that General Johnston is on his way here with 50,000 reinforcements. Life goes on here as it always has. Elise, dear, sometime next week, the military regiment will have a ball. I want to carry you and Jack to Madame Cognaisse's shop for fittings."

"Not me, Aunt Sissy," Jack spoke up, "I may not even go...to the ball, I mean."

"Oh, yes, Jack, dear," his aunt said, "I've told several of the girls around your age that you will be there. They want to meet you."

Jack's young face brightened at this news. "Well, I may go, but I don't want any new clothes, if I do go. Thanks, anyway,

Aunt Sissy."

"Well, I'll bet Elise won't turn down a fitting for a new dress, will you, dear? Before her niece could answer, she continued, "I saw a lovely dress at Madame Cognaisse's place. She's only had it a few weeks...it's straight from Paris, you know. I asked her to save it for me, so you could try it on. I want you to wear it to the ball. It will be especially beautiful with your dark hair and fair complexion. I know several young men of good families, who are looking forward to meeting you, also."

Emitting a little laugh, Elise hugged her aunt again and kissed her cheek. "I will try it on for you, Aunt Celia. I know it is lovely, if you think it is."

"Oh, it is, dear...straight from Paris! There won't be another one like it in town. We must go tomorrow for you to be fitted for it. You know, New Orleans is in enemy hands now... captured just a few weeks ago, so we won't be getting any more fashions from Europe...at least not until the war is over." Her aunt hesitated, then said she wanted to carry them to Sky Parlor Hill early in the morning to see the bluecoats on the river with the spyglass there.

Alan Holmes spoke up and said he knew that everyone was tired. He had to return to his regiment, but he welcomed all three of them to Belle Voir. He knew they all would be safe in Vicksburg. Smiling as he opened the front door, he waved to all of them and Elise realized that the tethered horse outside was waiting for her uncle.

Chapter Two

A rooster crow heralded the early morning, and Elise stretched in the spacious feather bed, wide awake. In the morning light, she looked around the large room, remembering the wallpaper with its motif of pink roses, some which were fully open and others with only tiny buds. Pink ribbons trailed through the flowers which had green leaves and stems with thorns. The colors were lovely against an ivory background. She noticed the large painted armoire with its beveled mirror, which her aunt had said was Louis XVI furniture. Its door was ajar, and she could see her homespun and other dresses hanging inside. The lovely French Provincial dressing table stood in front of another wall, and in the corner was the marble-topped washstand, just as she remembered. She realized then that Chloee, Old Scipio's wife, had come in during the early morning hours and had hung her dresses and petticoats in the armoire. Sighing with appreciation, she stretched again, with the happy thought that her life was returning to normal in Vicksburg. For the time being, she erased from her mind the soldiers on the train, the urgency and chaos at the depot, and the fact that almost all of her aunt's servants had left her.

Easing out of bed, she walked over to the window which offered a panoramic view of Belle Voir and all of its flowers and its outbuildings. She remembered the pale pink flowers of the plums and the yellow clustered flowers of the sassafras which were in full bloom, along with the garden violets and the quaint tiny heartsease. Yellow jonquils and the smaller flowered narcissus bloomed profusely in the spring awakening of the home. The grounds with their natural creeks and springs were the same, as she remembered.

The overseer's house stood empty, its occupant in the trenches with all of the other able men of the town. His wife had gone to a safer place, once the war began, her aunt said. The cookhouse was at the end of a covered walkway, but the cooks had fled over to the Yanks' side, as her Aunt Celia had told them the past evening, riding on a raft across the river. Now, only Chloee, old Scipio's wife, remained, to do any cooking.

Elise looked at all of the other forsaken outbuildings…the pantry, the carriage house, the smokehouse, the chicken house, the ice house, the milkhouse, the covered wells, and she remembered the cistern which was on the back porch of the main house. Fresh water was always available at Belle Voir. Some of the outbuildings had bullet holes and splintered wood as evidence of the constant shelling of the city. She wondered whether the main house had been hit, and she knew without a doubt that it had. She dreaded seeing it in the light of day. Hearing a knock at the door, she turned around. "Come in," she said.

"Good mornin', Miz 'Lise," Chloee said with a smile as she opened the door.

"Good morning, Chloee," Elise said, smiling and moving across the room to greet her.

"My, but you has growed!" Chloee said as she gave Elise a hug.

"I'm a grown woman now, Chloee," Elise said with a smile and a slight toss of her head.

"Ah b'lieves you is, Miz 'Lise," Chloee said, adding, "an' sech a bootiful lady! Lawd a' mercy, but you has growed!"

"Thank you, Chloee. You and Sip seem about the same - not much difference in three years' time. You're the same sweet Chloee." Chloee beamed at this before announcing that breakfast was ready.

"I'll be down soon, Chloee. Thank you for hanging my dresses in the wardrobe."

"Yes'm...Sip brung yo baggage in last night an' ah hung yo dresses an' put yo other clothes and bonnets in de drawers. De bonnet boxes is under de bed. Ah try to be quiet, since you wuz fast asleep, and ah knowed you wuz tired." Chloee turned to leave but then offered to style Elise's hair for her. Elise was pleased at this, for she knew that Chloee, along with others of her color, had been trained in New Orleans to style their mistresses' hair in the latest fashion.

Elise sat at the dressing table, looking into its matching mirror, while Chloee parted her hair in the middle, then pulled her hair sleekly across the back of her head, braiding it in several rows across the nape of her neck. Over this, she secured a hairnet. This seemed appropriate for a daytime carriage ride and visit to Sky Parlor Hill. Happy with the result, Elise thanked her and promised to be down for breakfast within a few minutes.

After dressing in a petticoat and homespun dress, Elise descended the stairs to the dining room where she could hear low voices. When she entered the room, she saw her mother and brother already seated at the table and her aunt slipping into her seat at the large dining room table. Old Sip and Chloee were serving breakfast.

"Did you sleep well, Elise?" her aunt asked.

"Oh, yes, Aunt Celia," Elise replied. Her mother and brother affirmed what she said. They had slept well, also. Their breakfast consisted of fresh bread, eggs, bacon and fruit. Elise realized her aunt was attempting to live her life as she did before the war. Her only concession to the privations of the war, as Elise noted, was the dour homespun dress she wore. Almost everyone now in the South wore homespun, including President Davis, himself. It was worn as a badge of honor. As they ate their breakfast, Celia Holmes asked her servants how much food was left in the pantry.

"Dis be de las' of de coffee, Miz Sissy," Chloee said. "Dar's bacon in de smokehouse but ah don' know but what de soldiers mighta took it. Dey took all de hawgs, as you knows."

Elise stared at the French china and silver on the table. Maybe things were not as bad as Chloee's words made them to be. The heavy draperies in the parlor and the dining room were the same that she remembered from several years prior, along with the buffet and sideboard and china cabinet. She glanced at her aunt who sat calmly eating her breakfast.

"Well, if all the coffee is gone, we will have Confederate coffee tomorrow. Don't we have some sweet potatoes left in the pantry, Chloee?" Not waiting for an answer from her servant, she continued, "That's what everyone is drinking now…sweet potato coffee. We can make do, too," Celia Holmes said before adding, "By the way, Alan sent me word early this morning that General Pemberton is ordering noncombatants, which include you three and myself, also, to leave Vicksburg."

"But we just got here," Elise said, looking at her mother and brother.

"I know you did, dear, and I personally think you'll be safer here. I'm not leaving, either. I'm just repeating what Alan said. Alan also said you will be safer here than in Jackson. Alan said the railroad will be torn up sometime within the next few days. Wade and the boys need to come on! He encourages you to stay here in Vicksburg with us!" Before anyone answered, Celia Holmes deftly changed the subject.

"Scipio is going to bring our carriage around after breakfast. I want you all to see the federal ships which are not far up the river. We'll go up to Sky Parlor Hill and you can use the spyglass there to look at them."

After quickly swallowing his toasted bread, Jack said, "I was wanting to find us some vegetables and fruit, Aunt Sissy. You said the crops are rotting in the fields."

"Well, goodness gracious, I was wanting you three to see the federal boats on the river. We'll go to Sky Parlor Hill and you can look through the glass there, but if you want to wait on your Uncle Alan to take you, Jack, that'll be fine. He'll enjoy taking you up there."

Jack wavered at this revelation but finally said he would go later to the hill. He wanted to see the Union troops but he would go later with his Uncle Alan. Everyone smiled, for they knew that Jack wanted to enlist in the Confederate army, and Elise knew her brother would discuss this with his uncle. After all, their father would okay such a thing if his brother agreed to it, but Elise feared what her mother would do, if such occurred.

After breakfast, Celia asked Scipio to bring the carriage to the front drive. They would go to Sky Parlor Hill before going to Madame Cognaisse's shop, she said. Scipio left to get the carriage as Chloee cleared the table.

"Jack, we still have our mule, CoCo, if you want to ride around," his aunt said. "Sip will bring us back this afternoon, and you two can look for vegetables then. You'll find a saddle in the stable. You may want to ride down to see your friend, Tommy. He may have persuaded his father to let him fight. He's barely sixteen now, I understand."

"Thank you, Aunt Sissy. I want to fight, too, but Papa won't let me." Jack scowled at this, but his aunt said she thought he was too young, also, at the age of fourteen.

As Jack left to saddle the mule, Elise and her mother went upstairs to get their wide-brimmed hats. However, Abby changed her mind, saying that she wasn't feeling well and would rest, instead. She stopped at her bedroom door, breathing hard, saying she was going to lie down. Elise had expected this, as her mother was in frail health and often lay down during the day.

Waiting for Scipio to bring the carriage to the front door, Elise walked with her aunt to the circular driveway, then turned around and looked at the two-story house which had been built with slave labor, its rosy brick even more lovely with age. Yes, it had bullet holes, as she had suspected. Several pieces of wood had been ruined, along with some of the wrought iron on the old house. Celia Holmes had tears in her eyes as she told Elise when most of the damage had occurred. Scipio arrived with the horses and carriage, then climbed down to assist both ladies into the carriage.

Seated in the landau with her aunt, Elise gazed at the town of Vicksburg as Scipio guided the horses to Sky Parlor Hill. She had heard about the caves being dug but since the dugouts were facing east, they weren't apparent from the main street. Her Aunt Celia promised to take her to see them later. Near the river's edge were the Confederate batteries which she had seen the past evening. She could see three Union gunboats now, upriver near the De Soto Peninsula. As her aunt pointed them out to her, several shells flew from the boats, making them duck involuntarily in the carriage. Elise was beginning to wonder, after all, whether they would be safe in Vicksburg. It was certainly not the city that she remembered.

Elise looked around the town and countryside as Scipio drove them on toward Sky Parlor Hill. Flowers were blooming everywhere, the air heavy with the perfume of honeysuckle and jasmine. Fruit trees were laden with their bounty of apricots and the beginnings of June apples. However, the trees and gardens and houses were riddled with bullets and shells which wouldn't let one forget that Vicksburg was at war.

"Alan hired some Negroes to build us a cave," her aunt said, patting her niece's knee. She said this easily, without any emotion, but Elise sensed a chill in the air.

"He talked to Sip about digging one, but Sip's too old, and we need him in the house, anyway. However, Sip knew the Negroes who dug the cave last week. Some of them are making good money, digging the caves. The caves are on the east side of town, since the shells are coming to us from the gunboats on the river. I understand some families have actually moved into the caves."

"Moved into the caves?" Elise asked with a surprised and worried look on her face, remembering the dim lights in the caves which she had seen from the train.

"Yes, dear, but it's only temporary. The war will be over soon, and everything will return to normal. Don't you worry about anything. We're all going to be fine. Oh, we're already at Sky Parlor Hill."

Elise hadn't realized that the horses had pulled the carriage to the foot of the hill which was supposed to be the highest point in Vicksburg, likely three hundred feet above the river. Her aunt explained that the balcony around the cupola of the newly built courthouse and Hansford's Hill were other vantage points for viewing the enemy on the river, but they were not as safe as Sky Parlor Hill. In fact, the courthouse was a favorite target of the Union soldiers who constantly shelled it. After all, she said, the courthouse was built with slave labor, and this intensified the Yankees' shelling.

As Scipio waited below with the horses and carriage, Elise and her aunt began climbing the wooden steps to the top of the hill. As they climbed the steep and dizzying flight of steps, Elise thought about the difference between her mother and her Aunt Celia. Though they were close in age, her mother's health was fragile, whereas her older sister's was robust.

Elise At Vicksburg

After reaching the top of the steps, her aunt reminded Elise that they were several hundred feet above the river and had a bird's-eye view of the river and the peninsula and the Louisiana side of the Mississippi River. In the distance ahead, Elise saw cultivated fields, some already yellow with grain. A small band beside them on the hilltop began playing "Dixie" as her Aunt Celia found the large field glass and looked up the river before handing it to Elise. As Elise looked through the spyglass, listening to the jaunty strains of the Southern song which the Confederacy had adopted as its own, she could feel the pride and could imagine the certain victory of the South that she loved.

However, seeing the federal encampment up the river and on the opposite, Louisiana shore, with its white tents and soldiers in blue uniforms moving about with obvious confidence and ease, she felt an uneasiness that lingered and would not go away. She saw tugboats apparently carrying dispatches from one gunboat to another and couriers galloping from tents to other encampments. When the last notes of "Dixie" died away, she could hear the responding song "When Johnny Comes Marching Home Again," played by the Union musicians, its lively tune wafting across the great river. As the music faded away, she heard gunshots fired from the ironclads on the river.

As Elise and her aunt stood there in the slight breeze of the summit, several shells from the gunboats below fell not far from where they were standing. Startled, Elise laid down the spyglass and her aunt urged her to go down the steps and get into the carriage. As they neared the bottom of the steps, a shell exploded and pieces from it stuck in the flagstone near the steps. Frightened, both of them were soon in the carriage and on their way into town. The next stop was Madame Cognaisse's shop for Elise's dress fitting.

The horses pulled the carriage down the long incline,

reminding Elise of the unusual topography of Vicksburg. One either traveled up or down because of the city's deep ravines. It was this incredible lay of the land that made the town seemingly unconquerable.

In the distance Elise saw what looked like a camel approaching them. She laughed out loud as the animal neared them, its splayed feet and knobby knees adding to the spectacle. Elise laughed again as her aunt told her that the camel had been adopted by the Rebel soldiers who named it "Old Douglas." Though the camel had been tethered numerous times, it always broke loose, so it was allowed to roam and graze freely. Besides being the army's mascot, especially the mascot of Company A of the 43rd Mississippi Regiment, it often carried instruments and knapsacks of the regimental band. Old Scipio gave the miscreant camel a wide berth as it clopped past the carriage, for the horses shied away from the humped animal.

As Scipio guided the Percherons to the dress shop, Elise thought it remarkable that the renowned store was still open. So many of the town's businesses were closed and shuttered. The lovely shop not only housed fine merchandise but also it was a beacon of normality which would soon return to the entire town, once the war was over and the South had won.

After leaving the dress shop, and now seated in the carriage again, Elise thought about the dress she would be wearing to the upcoming ball. Made of thin white muslin over an underdress of delicate blue silk, the dress worked its charm on her imagination. However, though it was beautiful, the important thing in her mind was that it meant that life was returning to normal, that her life in Vicksburg was a return to the way things used to be. She felt a sense of true relief, and a smile appeared on her face. Needing a few nips and tucks for a true fit, according to the engaging Madame Cognaisse, the dress remained at the French woman's shop with the promise that it would be ready for her before the time of the ball.

"The dress looks lovely on you, dear," her aunt said, nudging Elise from her reverie.

"Oh, I love it, Aunt Celia! You have always been so good to me, and I love you!" Elise leaned over and kissed her aunt on her cheek. "Thank you so much!"

"You are the daughter I never had," her aunt said with a twinkle in her eyes and a light kiss on her niece's forehead, before settling back for the carriage ride.

Old Scipio flipped the reins over the horses' backs and urged them forward with a gruff "Git up dar!" As Scipio turned his head, Elise could see the chaw of tobacco in his jaw, something that would certainly meet with her aunt's disapproval, and when he leaned over to spit over the side of the carriage, she looked at her aunt, expecting a sharp reprimand. However, none was forthcoming, and Elise remembered what her aunt and uncle had told them the evening before…things were not as they used to be. Colored servants pretty much did as they pleased now and the relationship between servant and master had changed. Her aunt had said that Sip and Chloee hadn't yet rafted across the river to join the Yankees, as many of the slaves had done. However, it had not been easy, she had said, adjusting to things as they were now.

Elise glanced at the courthouse on the hill which was a focal point of the town. The large Confederate flag, mounted on its cupola, billowed slowly in the slight breeze, its circle of seven stars and red and white bars taunting the enemy. As shells from the ships on the river soared above their carriage toward the beleaguered courthouse, Elise could hear the sweet chirping of songbirds as they flew to and from their nests of eggs. It's strange, she thought, that life goes on as usual among the small creatures of nature, even during the violent disruptions of war, and for some reason, this brought a measure of comfort to her. As Elise wondered about the usual routines of nature during the ongoing war, the large courthouse clock chimed the midmorning hour of ten o'clock.

Yellow flags flew over the hospitals in town. Her aunt told her that there were two types of hospitals in town – one for the sick and the other for the wounded. Of course, she said, many of the homes harbored the sick and the wounded and these also had yellow flags flying over them. She said the prisoners of war were treated for their wounds before being housed in the prison downtown, where they would stay until after the war. Elise was surprised to hear that the top floor of the beautiful Duff-Green mansion was being used as a hospital for wounded Union prisoners, while the middle floor housed the Confederate wounded. The reasoning was that the bluecoats wouldn't shell the Duff-Green House, knowing their compatriots were housed on the top floor.

After a short silence, Elise heard her aunt's voice again, prodding her from her thoughts about how the war had wrought so many changes. "I told Sip to take us to see the caves first, then he'll take us to Drusie's house. I've put a few things in our cave. You'll see." Her aunt talked on, giving Elise the feeling that she wanted her to feel safe in Vicksburg.

"I saw Isabel Davis last week. She said for us to come by for a visit, so I told Sip we'd stop by after looking at our cave. The caves are on the east side of town, facing away from the Yankee shells. I had some chairs and rugs and a few pictures put on the walls of our cave, so maybe it will be a little more like home."

Elise didn't know what to say. Her aunt was so calm and matter-of-fact. What would they do for water and other necessities? She managed a half smile and her aunt patted her knee.

"We'll be fine, dear one. Scipio will bring us water from

the cistern in the house, and he and Chloee can bring us food from the market place in town. The war should be over soon. Vicksburg will never be taken. You and Abby and Jack are safe here. I want Wade and Mark and Jeremy to catch the next train to Vicksburg. The Yankees will take Jackson soon, if they haven't, already."

Scipio guided the horses up the nearest cobblestone street which led to the eastern side of Vicksburg. It was a rocky ride as the horses' hooves slid into the crevices of the cobblestones for surer footing. They pulled together up the steep hill, throwing the occupants of the carriage from side to side. Elise had never noticed the topography of the land of Vicksburg as much when she was younger and visiting. However, being older, she realized that one either rode, or walked, up or down, never on even ground, for it was a land of steep embankments which were covered with trees and deep ravines, grown up with cane and underbrush. These incredible land features had kept Grant and his minions at bay for over a year now.

Reaching one of the many narrow ledges where caves were dug into the clay earth, all on different strata of the hills, Scipio guided the horses past the rows of hollowed-out caverns, until he came to a freshly dug one which, Elise assumed, belonged to her aunt and uncle. As the horses slowed to a halt, Celia attempted to give her niece directions from the cave to the back porch of her house which was directly up the embankment, above the cave. In other words, she said, if the shelling got worse, they would come down to get to the cave and climb up to get back to the house.

Without a horseblock to facilitate their exit from the carriage, Elise and her aunt alternately held to the side of the carriage and, with Scipio's assistance, eased to the ground. Elise gazed at the dark hollow that was the entrance to the cave, and she felt a terrifying dread. As her aunt led the way into the cave, it was all she could do to keep from running back to the safety of the carriage.

"Come along, Elise," her aunt said, rummaging in her purse for a match to light the lantern that was near the cave's entrance. Elise guessed that maybe six or more feet of earth were above the opening of the dugout. What if it caved in? She almost panicked, just thinking about the possibility. However, with her aunt leading the way, holding the glowing lantern, Elise followed behind, her senses overpowered by the clayey smell of the dugout. She did her best to stifle a scream as she walked through the earthy tomb, realizing that they all might have to live in it for some time.

The ceiling in the main room of the cave was perhaps six or more feet in height. A large rug on the dirt floor and a few pictures on the walls, along with several chairs, a settee, and some small tables, gave the room a contrived homey effect. Niches carved into the clay wall held candles and books and small pictures. A small closet for provisions was dug into the wall of the cave. Elise's feelings of suffocation and nausea lifted slightly as her aunt turned to look at her and to urge her on to other parts of the dugout. Elise followed her, looking into each of several curtained rooms. There were four of these, her aunt said, one for her and her mother, one for Jack, one for her aunt and her uncle who would rarely be there, and one for Chloee and Old Sip. One room had a table and some chairs in it.

Pulling back the sheet curtain of the first dugout bedroom, her aunt said, "This is your and Abby's room. This is where you and your mother will stay if worse comes to worst, and we have to live in the cave. I put two cots in here and a table and chair. But, come on, dear, I want you to see the rest of our cave." Too traumatized to utter a sound, Elise managed a smile and nodded her head, as her aunt led her on through the cave.

Her aunt pulled back the makeshift curtains of each of the improvised bedrooms which held mattresses piled on top of other mattresses and several cots for beds. Each room also held a small table with a pitcher and basin for washing. A lidded chamber pot was another accessory in each of the bedrooms, and for the first time Elise could only imagine the indignities which they all would be forced to endure if they had to live in the caves.

Elise's mind was racing. She thought about the cistern on the back porch of her aunt's and uncle's home. Would Old Sip be able to climb up and down the hill between her aunt's house and the cave? Jack and Chloee, of course, could help him. They would need a large pail to fill with enough water for the bowls in the four rooms.

The realization that Vicksburg was preparing for all-out war in spite of well-meaning denials by her aunt, suddenly struck Elise, and she wondered what her mother would think about their underground refuge. She fought back tears as her aunt beckoned her on, wanting to show her the back part of the cave.

Elise was surprised to find that the cave was connected to other caves in the hill, and her aunt led her on to these hideouts, which were not yet occupied by their owners. On one side, her aunt explained, would be a young mother who had two children and was expecting her third child. Her husband had been killed several weeks before by a Minie ball, lobbed from the river. The other side would be occupied by an older man and his wife. These other families had servants and dogs and cats which would live in the caves with their owners.

"You're awfully quiet, Elise, dear," her aunt said. "I didn't want to frighten you, as we may never have to use this cave. We don't expect Vicksburg to fall, but if the fighting gets worse, we'll have somewhere to go." Her aunt suddenly ceased talking and held the lantern close to Elise's face.

"You're pale, child," she said. "Remember, we may never need this cave. You and your mother and Jack will be safe, regardless...and I forgot to tell you...your father and the two younger boys will stay in the room with Jack. We'll all be safe here. Now, let's go to see Drusie and Isabel. They have a cave near here, also, so I don't know whether they'll be in their cave or at home."

"I...it's actually better than I thought it would be, Aunt Celia," Elise said, trying to believe her own words. "You've done so much to make it livable," she added and was rewarded with a smile from her aunt whose comforting words dispelled her feelings of panic and suffocation and fear. Nevertheless, it was sheer relief to be back in the carriage again.

The horses had pulled the landau only a short distance down the narrow strip of land in front of the dugouts, when several people emerged from one of the caves ahead of them. Old Sip reined in the horses as Elise and her aunt simultaneously recognized their friends ahead.

"It's Drusie," Elise said, laughing.

"And Isabel and Tommy," her aunt added. "I guess Jack couldn't find Tommy at home because he was here in their cave. Sip, help us down, so we can speak to them."

The three members of the Davis family, startled by the appearance of the horses and carriage, suddenly recognized its occupants. Drusie led the way with outstretched arms to Elise who met her also with arms opened wide. As they welcomed each other with a laugh and hug, Isabel and Celia greeted each other as longtime friends who often visited each other. When Celia asked about her husband, Edward, Isabel said he stayed in the trenches now most of the time.

Tommy asked Elise about Jack, and she explained that he had probably tried to find Tommy at home, not knowing he was in their cave.

"Come on, Elise," Drusie said. "Let me show you our cave."

"It's our home away from home, Elise," Isabel Davis said. "Oh, I heard today that over 500 caves have been built now in Vicksburg. Everybody's calling them 'bombproofs.' Goodness gracious, let's hope they are!" she said.

"Yes, I've heard the same thing, Isabel," Celia Holmes said with a smile. "Thank you, but I think Elise has seen enough of a cave today. I just took her on a tour of ours. We'll see it another time, Isabel." Elise smiled and agreed that she would see theirs later, before turning to speak to Tommy.

"My, but you have grown, Tommy!" Elise said with a laugh, realizing that Drusie's brother had not taken his eyes off her. For the first time she could remember, Tommy Davis appeared to be awkward in her presence, while at the same time attempting to be mature and nonchalant.

Shuffling his feet and looking down at her from his new height, he asked about the rest of her family. Would they be coming to Vicksburg, also?

"Oh, yes, they should be here within a few days," Elise said.

"Elise, do you have your dress yet for the ball next week?" Drusie asked.

"Yes, Drusie, we just left Madame Cognaisse's shop. She has to alter it a bit for me. I want to see your dress, also. We'll see them at the ball next week."

"Oh, I can't wait!" Drusie said, laughing. "Yes, we'll see each other's dresses then."

"I took Elise to Sky Parlor Hill earlier this morning," Celia said, adding, "Abby wasn't feeling well, so she didn't go. Jack wanted to look for some fruit and vegetables, and he wanted to see you, Tommy, but he wanted to talk to Alan first, so he was to go to Alan's entrenchment. I told him to ride CoCo, so he may still be in town. I believe he's wanting to be in the trenches with Alan, but we all think he's too young. He's only fourteen."

"Oh, he's old enough, Mrs. Sissy," Tommy said, animatedly. "A lot of boys are younger than Jack...some just lie about their age and get away with it, because they're so needed. Others are allowed to help, regardless of their ages." Gone was Tommy Davis' unease while addressing Elise and in its place was a passion for the Confederacy. Elise observed this with amusement that no one else appeared to notice.

"Yes, Edward and Tommy stay in the trenches most of the time now. I didn't want Tommy to fight, but General Pemberton needs all who will fill in. I tell Edward to look after Tommy, and he does," Isabel said.

Elise spoke up, revealing that Jack had begged their father to let him fight, also, but their father wouldn't give his permission.

"As Tommy said," Isabel confided, frowning and shaking her head, "some are younger than Jack, but I agree with you. Jack's too young."

"Well, we must be going, Isabel," Celia said, turning toward the carriage. Elise followed her aunt, turning to wave goodbye as Scipio helped them into the carriage.

"The ball is only a few days from now," Drusie said, excitedly, "We'll see you then. We're all planning to go." Her mother, Isabel, echoed her words and added that she hoped Wade and the younger boys would arrive in time to go. Elise smiled as her aunt said that her father and the boys should arrive any day now, and they all planned to attend the ball.

As the horses pulled the carriage along the lengthy row of hollowed-out openings in the steep side of the embankment, Elise saw people carrying mattresses and cots and tables and chairs into the freshly dug caves. Many waved and called out greetings as they passed by, prompting them to reply with a nod and a smile and greetings of their own.

After breakfast several days later, Elise sat in the parlor

with her aunt and mother, making bandages and lint and cartridges for the home regiments. The lint was carefully scraped from Celia Holmes' table linens and pillow cases. Bandages were made from rolls of linen from her bed linens. Several nearby neighbors dropped by and found seats in the parlor where they, too, joined in making what their local units needed. After finishing their morning work, they all went to Sky Parlor Hill to view the federal gunboats and ironclads up the river below and to watch the bluecoats on-board with their spyglasses, focused on the town above them.

When they returned home, Alan Holmes was there. As he related to them the progress of the war, Jack came down the stairs, wearing a gray Confederate uniform. Abby stood up with tears streaming down her cheeks and reached out to her son who stooped down and kissed her cheek.

"Don't do this to me, son," she sobbed. "You're too young. Remember what your father said. Please spare me this worry and fear," she cried.

"Mama, General Pemberton needs us. I'll be okay. I'll stay near Uncle Alan," Jack said.

Alan hurriedly interjected, "I'm watching out for him, Abby. This war won't last long. Grant's been trying for over a year now to get to Vicksburg and failed. Vicksburg will never be taken!"

Finding a handkerchief in her pocket, Abby held it to her eyes and, still weeping, left the parlor. Elise found her mother later in her room, sitting on the side of her bed and sobbing uncontrollably. As Elise sat beside her mother and put her arms around her shoulders, Abby spoke in a trembling voice.

"I wish we hadn't come to Vicksburg, Elise! I believe we're in greater danger here than in Jackson."

"Mama, it won't be long before Papa and the boys will come. Uncle Alan says Jackson is in greater danger than

Vicksburg," Elise said.

"Well, why don't they come on? I wish Wade would forget about hiding the silver. I know he has to sell the rest of the cattle," Abby said, her voice breaking, "as they have to be fed. Oh, Elise, I don't know whether Cuffey and the other servants are still with them or even whether the train is still running from Jackson to Vicksburg."

When a light knock sounded at the door, Celia and Alan and Jack all entered. Celia sat on the bed by Abby and put her arms around her sister.

Alan Holmes stood before Abby, his military kepi in his hands. Jack stood by him with an anguished look on his young face. Alan was the first to speak.

"Abby, I'm looking after Jack. He's a courier for General Pemberton. Just about all of the boys his age and younger are helping us in some way. We need him, Abby."

"Mama, please don't worry about me," Jack said, and for the first time, Elise noticed the beginnings of a beard on her brother's face. Jack bent down and kissed his mother before continuing.

"Vicksburg will never be taken, Mama. They told me that ol' Grant's been trying for over a year to capture Vicksburg," he said with pride in his voice which now seemed deeper. Why, almost overnight, he had become a man, Elise thought. As Abby wiped her eyes again and sighed, looking down at the floor, Alan Holmes kept trying to reassure her.

"Wade and Mark and Jeremy should go ahead and ride the train to Vicksburg," he said. "I sent a letter to Wade, but I've been told it was intercepted by some of the northern troops that are on the outskirts of Jackson. I urged him in the letter to go ahead and make the trip with the boys to Vicksburg, but there's no way I can contact him now. It's a matter of a few days before Jackson falls, anyway, I've been told. It won't be long before they tear up the railroad tracks, if they haven't already done so."

Noticing that everyone in the room looked upset, Alan added some words of reassurance.

"General Johnston is on his way to Jackson with 50,000 men. We have six roads and one railroad entering our city, and all of them are defended by our nine forts. We're just waiting on Johnston."

Celia rose from the bed beside Abby, saying that she had to talk to Chloee and Sip about dinner. As everyone turned to leave, Celia told Abby that she should rest and that Chloee would bring her dinner up the stairs to her.

Chapter Three

The military ball was in progress at the lovely Balfour home, and everyone hoped and prayed it would not be a repetition of all that happened earlier, only a few weeks past. Then, as if the Yanks had been tipped off, Grant had ordered his gunboats to begin their torturous passage down the Mississippi, before the rebel batteries, and the sounds of cannon and shells brought an end to the dancing and merrymaking. This evening was another attempt to restore life as it once was before the bluecoats across the river began shelling their beloved city. Regardless, however, the residents and soldiers at the ball now were on high alert, but trying not to let the sounds of war drown out the music of the regimental orchestra.

Having arrived only a few minutes earlier, Elise and Drusie sat on a rose velvet-covered settee in the large ballroom, tapping their dancing shoes to the military orchestra's rendition of "Dixie." After catching up on their lives during the past few years, when they had not visited with each other, Drusie commented on Elise's hair.

"Did Chloee give you the latest New Orleans hairdo, Elise?"

"I suppose she did, Drusie. It's called 'cats, rats, and mice,'" Elise said, laughing.

"Oh, you do have the latest. I've heard of it. It's all the rage, but I've never had my hair fixed like that. Oh, I do like it!"

"Thank you, Drusie, but I couldn't help but laugh when Chloee told me what it was called. She was laughing, also." When

Elise complimented Drusie's long coiffure and Drusie called it the "waterfall" look, they both laughed at that, also. Elise commented that she was glad she thought to bring the hair rats with her when they came to Vicksburg, hair which she had saved for some years when she brushed her hair. Drusie commented that she had saved hers, also. Elise could only think how wonderful it was to be at the ball with Drusie and to be laughing, as they always did when they were together.

Elise looked around the room and saw her brother, Jack, surrounded by several young girls. He had decided at the last minute that he would go to the ball, and Elise was certain that he attended because he wanted to wear his new Confederate uniform. Tommy Davis was also in the group with Jack, and he, too, had on his uniform.

The large ballroom was decorated with Confederate flags placed on stands around the room and Confederate bunting which adorned the walls. As the clapping and shouting died down, following the battle song, an aide to General Pemberton mounted the dais to address the enthusiastic partygoers. Dressed in Confederate gray, he tapped on a nearby chair in the orchestra section to get everyone's attention. All talking and laughter ceased as couples on the dance floor returned to seats around the walls of the ballroom. In the silence that followed, the aide spoke loudly and swiftly.

"General Pemberton and I welcome you to our regimental ball which we have been planning since the last one. Let's make sure that this one doesn't end the way the last one did. As you recall, Grant must have been tipped off about the party because he chose that night to move his gunboats past our batteries on the river. The cannon and the shells caused such a ruckus that we had to end the party.

"Ladies and gentlemen," he continued on a different note,

"Vicksburg is a safe place to be. Lincoln says our city is the key to victory for the bluecoats, and the north can't claim victory until that key is in his pocket. Well, we don't plan to give him the key to our fair city!" He paused for a few moments, looking around the crowded ballroom, as laughter and clapping erupted.

"Ladies and gentlemen, let's all have a good time! Let's show the Yanks that we're having a good time in Vicksburg and they won't ever get to our city!" Once again, the large room erupted in clapping, this time accompanied by the murderous rebel yell from the large number of soldiers present.

As the general's aide left the dais, the dance master of the evening appeared in the middle of the ballroom and asked the ladies to look at their dance cards. The dances were listed on their cards, but the first one, the Grand March Medley, would include only two, "Darling Nellie Gray" and "The Girl I Left Behind Me." The dance master then offered to help any couples who needed instruction about the dance steps. Seeing that no one wanted assistance, he said loudly, "Ladies, see that your dance cards are filled out, then let the dancing begin!"

Elise was breathless with excitement and was surprised but pleased when a line of young men formed before her, along with her Uncle Alan who would introduce each one. She was amused to see Tommy Davis first in line, proudly wearing his gray uniform. Since he needed no introduction, Elise removed the dance card from her wrist where it had been attached with a braided cord and gave it to Tommy. Producing a stub of a pencil from his pocket, his face flushed red, Tommy wrote his name on several lines of the card. He then stood by Elise, expecting to have the first dance with her, as other young men affixed their names to her dance card. Elise recognized some of these as soldiers on their train trip from Jackson to Vicksburg.

The dance master urged all couples interested in the Grand

March to meet him on the dance floor. He then nodded to General Pemberton and his wife, Patty, to lead the march. As the general and his wife moved to the dance floor, Tommy Davis awkwardly crooked his right arm which Elise accepted lightly with her gloved finger tips. She was so excited and happy about dancing again that she made up her mind not to notice Tommy's probable ineptness as a dance partner.

Following the lead of the general and his wife, couples began marching to the beat of the music, being careful to keep the line of march unbroken and the couples at uniform spaces from one another. Elise noticed that General Pemberton appeared to be quite familiar with the march and the different evolutions of the dance steps. He appeared not to be bothered by the shrieks of the shells and weaponry that bore down upon the grounds of the Balfour House from the Federals, only a few miles up the river from Vicksburg. As Elise concentrated on the changing dance steps, she realized her young partner was talking to her.

"You're beautiful, Elise," Tommy Davis said earnestly, his boyish face grinning with appreciation as he looked down at her. Before she could answer, he complimented her dress and the flowers which formed a tiara of sorts in her hair. At her aunt's request, Chloee had picked some flowers from her untended and shell-riven gardens for Elise's hair.

Smiling up at him, Elise murmured a thank you, realizing that someday he might break some woman's heart, but not now…not hers. However, she had had enough beaus in her eighteen years of life to know that Tommy Davis, at the age of sixteen was completely captivated with her. Though she felt somewhat flattered, she certainly did not share his feelings. He was her best friend's younger brother, and that was all.

Her eyes sought out Drusie and her dancing partner who were near the end of the long line of couples, which had wound its way around the wall on the opposite side of the room. Drusie returned her gaze with a smile, and Elise knew there would be a time soon when she would have to nip in the bud any courting relationship with her brother. After all, he was still a child and she a grown woman.

When the Grand March was over, Alan Holmes appeared at Elise's side to introduce the young men whose names were on her dance card. One by one, she was escorted to the middle of the ballroom floor where she danced the night away, reveling in the feelings of freedom and safety and normalcy. Comments from others about her hair and her gown and her beauty made her heady because she had been denied these yearnings of youth during the years of war-mongering in Jackson. As the music swelled to a crescendo, she closed her eyes and gave herself to its rhythm, remembering her dance lessons which seemed, in retrospect, to have prepared herself for just this special occasion.

Suddenly, a deafening volley of cannon and shells burst near the Balfour House, making the house shake and the candles and lanterns flicker around the room. Though everyone stopped dancing and stood still, momentarily, looking fearfully at one another, they quickly returned to the dancing and fun of the evening. As Elise danced with the last soldier on her dance card, she noticed a man she had never seen, standing on the sidelines and dressed in the full uniform of the Confederacy. Added to his uniform was a red silk sash, worn from his right shoulder and tied at his left side.

Something about the man riveted her attention, and she felt a shiver of pleasure course through herself when he turned and looked directly at her. As they held each other's gaze, the dance director abruptly returned to the dais and rapped for the music to cease and for everyone's attention. He said that someone had requested, as a fun feature of the evening, the game Le Miroir, and the gentleman who requested it also had chosen Miss Elise Holmes to hold the mirror.

Elise's heart was beating rapidly as couples returned to their places around the walls of the large room. She had heard of the ballroom game, and had seen it performed, but had never participated in it. As someone brought a brocade-covered chair and placed it in the middle of the dance floor, the dance manager hurried over to Elise and asked if she would be willing to play the game.

"Yes," she said with a smile, trying not to let her voice betray her excitement, as the dance manager led her to the chair and motioned for her to sit in it. After she sat down, someone brought her a large mirror with a gold handle. Now, she thought to herself, she remembered how the game was played.

As the valse or waltz music filled the grand ballroom, she held the mirror so that she could see behind herself. One by one, young men moved across the dance floor to stand behind her chair, each one grinning broadly, hoping that she would choose him to dance this special dance of the evening. Repeatedly, she either smiled and shook her head or turned the mirror over to denote her denial of choosing any of them. Finally, after many declines, and much laughter, Elise once again looked into the mirror, behind herself, and was startled yet strangely pleased, to see the soldier who had held her gaze from the periphery of the dance floor.

Elise felt her cheeks flush as, once again, his eyes locked with hers in the mirror. She didn't know what to do, as they had not been introduced to each other and he appeared to be older and more mature than the other soldiers. She only knew that she was drawn to him and to his obvious interest in her – and her alone. She had not seen him on the dance floor during the entire evening. She also knew that if her mother had attended the ball, she would not have even played the mirror game. She knew that her mother, and probably also her aunt and uncle, would not only disapprove of the game but also this older soldier.

Once again, the room shook with the explosions of Minie balls and Parrott shells and cannon, lobbed from the gunboats up the river. As the candles and lanterns flickered, Elise felt a resolve building inside herself. Still looking at the stranger in the mirror, she felt her head nodding in approval and she saw a smile appear on his face.

A smattering of applause from the guests in the room and the swell of music from the orchestra brought Elise to her feet. As she handed the mirror to the dance manager and saw him remove the chair from the middle of the ballroom floor, she came face to face with the man she had chosen for the next dance. While rockets and Minie balls screamed overhead, almost muffling the orchestra's music, she was surprised to realize that at the age of eighteen she suddenly became fully aware that life was short and she needed to embrace it. It might not be around for long. She had a premonition inside her very soul that things were not all right in Vicksburg, regardless of the brave rhetoric of its soldiers and citizens. As other couples began moving to the dance floor, Elise saw her uncle only a few steps away, and she knew he was coming to introduce her to the unknown soldier she had chosen.

"Elise, honey, I would introduce this fine man, but I haven't yet had the pleasure of meeting him, myself." The soldier stepped forward, offering his hand to Alan Holmes.

"I'm Stone Jackson, sir," he said easily, first shaking Alan Holmes' hand, then turning to Elise, he nodded and spoke to her. Before Elise could answer, her uncle continued with the introduction.

"I'm Elise Holmes' uncle, Alan Holmes," he said before adding, "General Pemberton tells me you're an engineer and a graduate of West Point. We certainly need our engineers."

"Yes, well actually I left West Point but I did get my engineering degree later," Stone Jackson said, looking at Elise as if he were ready to join the dance already in progress. However, Alan Holmes persisted in his line of questioning, somewhat to Elise's amusement.

"You have a good southern name, almost the name of our general, Stonewall Jackson."

"Yes, well, actually, my name is Stonewall Jackson," he said, with an emphasis on the word "is." "He's a distant relative of mine."

"Oh? Well, it's good to meet you, Stone," Alan Holmes said before muttering to himself and to anyone else who might be listening, "it's a great Southern name, all right…well, I'll go and drink some more of Mrs. Balfour's wine and let you two enjoy the dance." Stone held out his hand and shook Alan Holmes' hand again, before he headed toward the wines on the refreshment table.

As Elise looked into her dance partner's eyes and felt his hand around her waist, she knew that a man held her, unlike the young boys she had danced with all evening. Vaguely, she wondered how old he was, and something told her that her mother and aunt and uncle would wonder why she denied the boys her age, who wanted to dance with her and, instead, chose this total stranger who was probably much older than she.

Throwing caution to the wind, she soon discovered that her partner could dance like none other she had ever known. As the soaring martial music of the "Radetzky March" filled the large ballroom, even as the enemy's rockets screamed outside, she felt safe in the arms of Stone Jackson. His faultless steps brought joy to the dance that she had never felt.

Several times during the dance, as she moved to the swell and rhythm of the music, she was lifted slightly from the floor, then effortlessly placed again on her feet. How could anything be wrong, she thought, with succumbing to the glorious strains of music and the remarkable finesse of her dancing partner? Something told her to enjoy this evening, for she might never again relish another one like it.

At times, the dance master began clapping his hands to the beat of the music, ostensibly to symbolize the sound of marching boots. All of the couples on the dance floor followed his lead, standing in place and clapping in rhythm until the music shifted to dance mode again. When this occurred, the couples separated, the ladies in their full-length ballroom gowns dancing away from their partners to the center of the dance floor. When the music changed again, they continued dancing as they returned to their partners who whisked them once more to the center of the large room.

Elise momentarily closed her eyes which were moist with repressed tears of joy and allowed Stone Jackson to maneuver her through the final steps of the martial music. Only after the music ended, and she glanced around, did she realize that other couples in the ballroom had stopped dancing and were watching her and her partner perform the final intricate dance steps. Somewhat embarrassed, she flushed as everyone applauded their dancing. Acknowledging that the dance had ended, Stone bowed to her and she returned his gesture with a customary curtsy.

The orchestra burst forth again with another rendition of "Dixie" as those in attendance began animatedly clapping and singing. Stone guided Elise back to her seat on the settee, then pulled up a chair and plied her with questions.

"May I see you again, Elise?"

"I...I don't know. My mother and brother and I are temporarily living with my aunt and uncle until the war is over," Elise said. "You met my Uncle Alan tonight. My family is from Jackson."

"Will your mother mind, if I come to see you?" Stone asked

earnestly, adding, "I realize I am a good bit older than you. Someone told me you are eighteen, right?" When Elise nodded her head, Stone continued. "Well, I'm all of 28, ten years older. Would your parents mind if I paid you a visit?"

"Oh, I would think not," Elise said, not really knowing what her parents would think about his visiting her. "My father and two younger brothers are due to arrive any day now on the train." She saw the expression on Stone's face change as he leaned toward her and placed one of his large hands over her folded ones in her lap. Puzzled, she looked at him, questioningly.

"I'm afraid it's too late, Elise," Stone said gently, "...the train is no longer running."

"Oh, no, don't tell me!" Elise said, her eyes brimming with tears. She quickly opened her small party purse and found a small, lace hanky which she held to her eyes. Why, oh why, she thought, hadn't her father gone ahead and made the trip to Vicksburg, before the tracks were torn up? With Stone doing his best to console her, Elise made a visible effort to control her tears and after a few minutes, noting that she was calmer, he abruptly changed the subject.

"I know where your aunt and uncle live, Elise," Stone said, adding, "It's probably the most beautiful place in Vicksburg."

"Thank you," Elise said. "I'll tell them what you said. I know they will be pleased."

"I mean it, Elise. I really admire it," Stone said. Elise then told him about the letter her uncle had sent to her father, urging him to take the next train to Vicksburg, only to have his letter intercepted by the northern troops between Vicksburg and Jackson.

"I'm sorry about that," Stone said. "It won't be long before Jackson falls."

Fresh tears rolled down Elise's cheeks, which she wiped repeatedly with her small handkerchief. She had her own questions to ask and she didn't let her tears stop her.

"Where are you from, Stone?" she asked.

"I'm from Kentucky," he said, pulling a folded handkerchief from his pocket and handing it to her.

"Thank you. I can't seem to control myself," she said as she accepted his handkerchief. "I guess I'm thinking about my mother when she hears that the train is no longer running from Jackson to Vicksburg. She isn't well," Elise said, her voice trailing to only a murmur.

"I want you to keep the handkerchief, Elise. I'm sorry your mother is not well, but you haven't answered my question: may I see you again?"

"I...I hope so," Elise said, hesitantly, not knowing what to say or what her mother would think about any of the evening's happenings. However, deep in her heart, she knew that she would see Stonewall Jackson again...and again. Before she could say anything else, however, her aunt and uncle stood before her, saying that the hour was late and they needed to check on her mother. It was time to go. They appeared not to notice Elise's tears nor the large handkerchief which she held in her hand.

Elise was preparing to leave when Drusie Davis appeared and said that she and her parents would bring Jack home, as he and Tommy were not ready to leave. They were still catching up on their lives during the past three years. Elise said that would be fine, and as she rose and said goodbyes to Drusie and others who came over to wish her and her family well, her uncle introduced her aunt and Stone Jackson to each other.

Celia Holmes commented that she had never seen anyone dance the "Radetzky March" the way he and her niece had done. Smiling, Stone bowed slightly and thanked her, saying he had never before had such a dancing partner, and he gave all the credit to Elise. Elise, of course, knew this wasn't so, but all she could do was shake her head in denial. No words came to her, for she was so thankful that her aunt and uncle did not appear to be disapproving about the mirror game she played nor the exuberant dance with a much older man. She breathed a sigh of relief.

During the carriage ride home, Elise related what Stone Jackson had told her about the capital city of Jackson falling and also about the train no longer running between Jackson and Vicksburg. Her uncle's only comment was that he had not yet received the news and could only guess that the engineers were the first to be informed. He also said it was indeed possible, as his letter had been confiscated by the Yanks. They each agreed not to tell Abby Holmes this latest news, as her health seemed to be deteriorating further and it would only add to her worries.

For days after the ball, Elise stayed busy, returning to the rituals of sewing and making bandages and cartridges in the mornings and carriage rides in the evenings. Her thoughts, however, were about Stone Jackson. She had heard that his relative and namesake, Stonewall Jackson, had died at the Battle of Chancellorsville. She wondered whether she would see Stone Jackson again. Would he come to see her? She had told her mother about him, but she didn't mention his age. Her ailing mother had said she had hoped Elise would meet a nice young man. This had been her only comment.

Their evening carriage rides always took them to Sky Parlor Hill, where they trained the spy glass on the enemy gunboats which were silhouetted like sentinels in the stream up the river from their lookout. The men on the boats appeared to be on picket or guard duty. In blue uniforms, with large spy glasses of their own under their arms, they constantly paced the decks of each ironclad, intermittently looking through the glasses and surveying the city towering above them in the near distance. There appeared to be many blacks on the boats.

One morning as Elise and her aunt and mother sat in the parlor, busy with their usual ritual of making needed items for their soldiers, Alan Holmes paid them a hurried visit. The ladies dropped what they were doing to hear about the latest news of the war. Dressed in uniform which was now wrinkled and worn, he first told them that Jackson had fallen and the train tracks destroyed between Jackson and Vicksburg. It would now be impossible for Wade and the two boys to come to Vicksburg. They had waited too long.

With a broken sob and a loud cry, Abby Holmes covered her face with her hands and wept. Elise's eyes were filled with tears as she put her arms around her mother and listened as her uncle told them the latest news of the war. Though Alan Holmes had always been confident and upbeat when talking about the war, he now seemed dejected and worried. Seeing Abby so upset, he wiped tears from his own eyes before continuing.

"Grant crossed the river at Bruinsburg Landing with 24,000 men and sixty field guns. Then, the rest of his army, under Sherman, crossed the river at Grand Gulf, bringing his force to over 45,000 men. How in tarnation did he do it? Only God knows how they made it by our entrenchments on the river. They've burned Warrenton and taken Raymond and are probably still in Jackson. If they come back to the east side of Vicksburg, I'm afraid Vicksburg will fall. As you know, all of our caves are on the east side! The caves will give you some protection, but you won't be as safe as when his army was across the river, attacking us from the West."

"One more thing before I leave," he continued, "we need cartridge bags for a weapon called the columbiad. The bags have to be made of flannel. Please pass this on to other ladies who are helping the war effort. I have some flannel shirts that can be used," he said, turning to his wife. Celia nodded her head in agreement, then quickly turned to Elise and Abby, suggesting that they all had flannel petticoats which could be used for the bags. Elise could only marvel at the resourcefulness of her aunt, as she and her mother, with tears still streaming from her eyes, agreed to donate their flannel petticoats to the war effort. Hearing this, Alan Holmes gave his wife a kiss on the cheek before hurrying out the front door, then mounting his horse and trotting through the front gate.

As her mother continued to dab at her eyes, Elise joined her Aunt Celia again in making needed items for their soldiers. Engrossed in her work, she happened to look out the front windows and was surprised to see a man in gray uniform, dismounting from a large black horse. Something about the powerfully built man was familiar, but she didn't recognize him until he walked to the front door, his gray hat held in one of his hands.

It was Stone Jackson! Elise had to restrain herself from running to the door to welcome him, but she quickly regained her propriety and walked to the door. Demurely, as her aunt and her mother watched her, Elise opened the door and looked into the dark brown eyes of the Confederate soldier. As their eyes met, Elise knew with a woman's certainty that Stone Jackson was as eager to see her as she was to see him. Yet, because of others present, they each performed a necessary charade of formality.

"Oh, do come in," Elise said, "and let me introduce you to my mother. You met my Aunt Celia at the ball recently." At this reintroduction, her aunt rose from her chair and welcomed him to her home.

"Thank you, Mrs. Holmes. I told Elise this is the most beautiful home in Vicksburg."

"Oh, she told me, Mr. Jackson. Thank you. We've all come upon hard times during the war, and it hasn't had the care it needs, but we hope it will survive the war."

At this, Elise interjected that she wanted him to meet her mother who was attempting to put her small handkerchief into her dress pocket. Stone moved easily toward her, at the same time pulling a letter from his shirt pocket.

"I am glad to meet you, Mrs. Holmes," he said, smiling as he handed the letter to her. "This is a letter from your husband, Wade Holmes."

Startled and surprised, Abby told him she was glad to meet him and appreciated his bringing her husband's letter to her. First, she read it through quickly before realizing that Elise and her sister were watching her, waiting to know what news was in the letter.

"Sister, does he have bad news?" Celia asked.

"Yes, he does," Abby said. "I want Elise to read it out loud, but first, I want to thank you again, Mr. Jackson, for bringing it to me." She said this, dabbing at tears rolling down her cheeks.

"You are welcome, Mrs. Holmes, but please call me Stone."

"Well, if you want me to, I will. Elise, please read what your father has to say," Abby said, handing the letter to Elise. Elise glanced at her father's handwriting, then read it out loud.

> "Dear Abby,
>
> I send you, and all, my love. Jackson is destroyed and almost everything burned to the ground. Our home remains intact, however, but the Yanks dug up every inch of ground, looking for our silver and china which I placed where they can't find them. Thank the Lord, we have our cistern and wells and clean water! Cuffey and our other servants joined the Federals when they entered Jackson. They also took our cattle and horses and carriage. The U. S. stars and stripes flag flies over our courthouse now. I don't know where General Johnston is. We heard he was in the area, but left

when Grant and Sherman arrived. We hear Johnston will come back, but when? We still have meat in the smokehouse and are eating it sparingly. A courier brought a letter from some of our Holmes cousins nearby, urging us to live with them until the war is over. I'm waiting until the Yanks leave to find someone with a carriage and horses, who can carry us there. I appreciate Mr. Stone Jackson, bringing me news that you all are safe and well and taking this letter back to you. Please thank him again for me.

All my love to you, Abby, to Elise and Jack, and to Celia and Alan,
Wade"

As Elise folded the letter and handed it to her mother, Abby took it and put it in her pocket, then holding on to Elise, she slowly walked to where Stone stood, his hat still held in his hands.

"You will never know how much I thank you, Stone," she said, her eyes still wet with tears.

"You are welcome, Mrs. Holmes," Stone said, adding, "I wanted to bring you the letter, and I also wanted to ask your permission to visit your lovely daughter."

Looking surprised, Abby said, "Oh, you must be the young man Elise was telling me about. "You…you are somewhat older than she…" Her voice trailed off to nothing.

"Yes, I'm afraid I'm ten years older, Mrs. Holmes, but I can't help that. I hope our age difference doesn't bother you."

Elise looked at her mother, breathlessly wondering what her answer would be. Her mother surprised her and also her aunt when she held out both hands to Stone and covered his outstretched hand with her own

"Stone," she said, "I can never thank you enough for bringing this letter to me from my husband. I don't know how you were able to do it, or what you went through to find my husband and to bring his letter back to us. I will never forget your kindness. You certainly have my permission to see Elise."

Thank you, Mrs. Holmes," Stone said as he helped Abby back to her chair. Then, nodding to Celia and Elise, he walked to the front door, with Elise behind him. Celia rose from her chair and thanked Stone for bringing the letter to her sister and invited him to come again to her home. He smiled and said he looked forward to visiting her and her family again. With Elise beside him, he walked through the large front door which he closed behind them.

"Thank God I'm free to see you again, Elise!" he said in a low voice, as they walked toward his horse.

"I think the letter from Papa did it," Elise said with a smile. "I don't know how you were able to go through the Union army without being detected. It was a dangerous thing to do," she added.

"Well, for one thing, I didn't wear my Confederate uniform," Stone said with a laugh. He stopped and put on his hat, and Elise asked about the insignia on the front of the hat.

"It's a castle with turrets," he explained. "It's an engineer's insignia."

"Oh, I didn't know," Elise said.

"Now, I need to know whether you would like to see me again," he said, with emphasis on the words "you" and "me." He looked down at her, and the only thing that kept her from throwing herself into his arms was the knowledge that they could be seen by those in the parlor of the large house. Elise knew that her eyes betrayed her when she looked up at him.

"I think you know that I would love to see you again, Stone, but I don't know how you can come to see me when the war is so close now. All of our soldiers will be engaged more and more, now that Vicksburg is encircled by the Yanks. We've been told to move into our cave, and I do dread it! I'm afraid it will be the death of my mother."

"I will help you all that I can," Stone said, as he mounted his horse.

"This is Blackberry," he said, introducing his horse to her as she ran her hand over the horse's velvet nose.

"Did you ride him to Jackson?" she asked

"I did," Stone said and added, "Take care of yourself, Elise. I'm coming again soon."

"Goodbye, Stone," she said. Tears brimmed in her eyes as the horse trotted away from her. At the gate, Stone turned and waved to her. At this, she held up her hand, and he was gone.

~ O ~

In the dark, early morning hours of the next day, Elise and her Aunt Celia and Jack sat in the Holmes' carriage, which Jack had enclosed by pulling the top forward, waiting as their routed army straggled down the main street of Vicksburg. Jack had awakened them the evening before. He had run from the Confederate entrenchments near the river with news from his uncle that in addition to Warrenton and Richmond, the towns of Port Gibson and Rocky Springs, the capital city of Jackson, and even Champion Hill had fallen. Several weeks before, they had seen the flames lick the sky from the small town of Warrenton, only a few miles south of Vicksburg. The blue devils had torched it.

"Retreat, retreat!" some of the men shouted in broken English as they trudged down the street with tears streaming down their faces, and Celia told Elise that they were Louisiana Acadians. Siege guns, gun carriages, and ambulances followed the demoralized army.

"We had to burn about 30,000 bushels of corn, since we didn't have transports to move it into the city," one of the soldiers volunteered with anguish to all who would listen.

From midnight until the early morning hours, the streets and roads of Vicksburg were jammed with the remnants of a defeated army. The Confederate troops had filled what wagons they had with turkeys, chickens, rice, corn, peas, and sugar. They had also rounded up dairy cows, beef cattle, hogs, sheep, and mules which they drove ahead of them. The mingled sounds of wagons, cannon, horses, mules, stock and sheep filled the air.

No order existed. As the hollow-eyed, footsore, exhausted army dragged themselves along the main thoroughfare, citizens with buckets of water hurried from nearby homes, offering water to the parched throats of the shattered army. Having filled several buckets of water from his aunt's cistern and placed them in the carriage, Jack carried these to the soldiers who drank profusely from them, thanking Jack as tears made rivulets through the dirt on their faces. Elise saw women standing by the street, waving their handkerchiefs and crying and calling out to the soldiers.

"You'll protect us, won't you? You won't retreat and bring the Yanks behind you, will you," they shouted, almost in unison.

A few of the straggling army managed to swing their hats and vow to die for the ladies, never to run or retreat, refusing to admit that they were now in retreat. Other poor fellows sat on their blankets or lay on the ground or leaned against trees…anything to rest their wearied bodies. They were silent and downcast.

Ambulances passed by with the wounded and dead. One bore the body of General Tilghman, his blood oozing slowly from the side of it. Dead wagons were making rounds of the many hospitals, bringing out the dead and carrying them to their long rest, north of the town in the city cemetery.

Seeing that his sister and his aunt were overcome with the horror of it all, with tears rolling unchecked down their cheeks, Jack hid his own tears and turned the carriage around, heading back to his aunt's home. Leaving the downtown area at early dawn, they could hear several bands on the courthouse hill playing "Dixie" and the "Bonnie Blue Flag." Loud, steady drum rolls followed these renditions, possibly to rally the shattered army. Elise was upset and shaken when her Aunt Celia fell on her shoulder, sobbing. She was not the stalwart aunt who had met them when they arrived from Jackson, who had said unequivocally that Vicksburg would never be taken.

    Elise felt in that moment that she herself was too young to bear the realization that Vicksburg might not be unconquerable, after all. She could see Jack shaking, as he held the reins of the horses, and she knew that he was crying, also. She needed someone, but who? It came to her that she had to be the one to give comfort, but how? She put her arms around her aunt and they held each other. She longed to comfort her young brother, also, but she knew that he was manfully trying to hide his tears, not wanting anyone to see them.

    As they made their way back to her aunt's home, Elise wondered how long the majestic old plantation could withstand the onslaught of cannon and shells. Many of the other lovely homes of the town had been targeted and burned by the steady fusillade of enemy powder and missiles. Some of the finest homes in the town had been demolished by their own regiments, so they would not obstruct their firing toward the enemy on the river below nor to their parapets east of the city.

    When they arrived back at the Holmes' estate, they saw several Yankee soldiers prowling around the back of the house. Elise had never seen a Yankee in full uniform, except the ones across the river, when she looked through the spy glass at Sky Parlor Hill. She was surprised that she felt no fear. She knew instinctively that they had come to steal. Jack helped his aunt from the carriage, then lent Elise a hand as she climbed to the ground.

Celia wasted not a moment in giving the robbers in blue a piece of her mind. With tears still wet on her cheeks, she accosted them.

"And what are you doing, young man?" she asked one of the Yankees, who had cornered one of her three remaining cows.

"We're looking for chickens, old woman," he replied, still holding on to one of the cow's horns.

"Well, let my cow alone!" she said. "You can have the chickens, but leave my cow alone!"

Elise looked at Jack in his gray uniform. She knew he didn't carry a weapon and was outnumbered.

"This is private property, Yanks! Don't come back!" Jack exclaimed.

"Better shut your mouth, boy!" one of the men said, moving menacingly toward Jack.

At this, one of the Union soldiers spied the chickens roosting on the tree limbs above and began grabbing them as they squawked and flapped their wings. The other two bluecoats began climbing the trees and ringing the necks of the protesting birds before throwing their carcasses into the sack of the one waiting below. With full sacks and smirches on their faces as they glared at Jack, the thieves left the premises. The Holmes' cow, vigorously shaking its head from side to side, and lowing, was left to live another day.

The events of that early morning resonated in Elise's mind several days later, when her Aunt Celia mentioned that she was going to help at one of the brigade hospitals. Remembering her aunt's tears following the defeat of their army only a few days before, Elise was surprised but pleased that her namesake had regained her feisty spirit in dealing with the escalation of the war. Elise immediately said she would go with her, and this brought a smile to her aunt's face. They decided to leave at once, before the shelling intensified.

At Celia's request, Sip had readied the horses and carriage. He offered to drive for her, but Celia told him she planned to drive the carriage herself. She then requested that he and Chloee should fill the large, clean buckets in the kitchen with water from the cistern on the porch and carry it to their cave. From the news reports from Alan Holmes, they would soon be living in their prepared cave. They would all need water in their different rooms of the cave.

Once in the carriage, Elise realized that the horses did not respond well to her aunt's verbal commands nor to her handling of the reins. Like other women all over the South, Celia Holmes was trying to learn to do things for herself…things she had never considered doing before the war. However, the horses were unused to a different driver, and they showed it. Her aunt finally handed the reins to Elise who had never driven a carriage either. Elise held the reins and attempted to cajole the large Percherons into doing her bidding. With her aunt giving her directions to Brigade Hospital No. 1, she drove the carriage into a ravine about a quarter of a mile behind the Confederate entrenchments. Many white tents holding the wounded and the dying dotted the valley floor.

Elise halted the horses near the large surgeon's tent, then dropped the reins and struggled to climb from the carriage without a horseblock to assist her. Next, she helped her Aunt Celia to the ground, before securing the horses at a nearby hitching post. She was grateful not to have had a major catastrophe in driving the carriage to the outlying hospital.

As they entered the improvised surgeon's tent, the agonized shrieks of pain and the muffled groans of the dying assailed them. The overpowering stench of blood and laudanum and the dirt mingled with blood beneath their feet were nauseating. They both were quickly put to work, holding knives and medicines for the attending doctors. Elise overheard two nurses who talked together, recounting the illnesses of the day which they had treated, including malaria, acute dysentery, gunshot wounds, and pneumonia. They also bemoaned the fact that their medicine was running out, with little left for others coming in. Their once-white uniforms were bloody and worn and they had the look of having never been washed. Their faces bore expressions of fatigue and sorrow and horror from all they had witnessed and borne.

Suddenly, another soldier was brought into the tent, who appeared to have been blinded by the missiles of the enemy. His arms were flailing on the sides of the litter as he attempted to rise from his prone position. Several volunteers tried to keep him from falling off the gurney.

"Where are you, boys? Oh, boys, where are you? Oh, I am hurt! Boys, come to me! God have mercy! Almighty God, have mercy!" He kept repeating his desperate questions, as some of the volunteers in the tent tried to soothe and reassure him. Finally, as he quieted down and slumped back on the litter, just as he closed his eyes in death, his last whispered words were "Mother... Mother...."

There was sometimes mercy in death, Elise thought as she saw her aunt reach into the pockets of her dark homespun dress for several medicines which she had brought from her home. The two nurses who had been discussing the shortage of medicines quickly grabbed the remedies and stashed them on a makeshift shelf near the surgeon's table. The patient on the table was about to undergo an amputation of his leg.

The surgeon slated to perform the amputation took a quick swallow of whiskey, then rolled up the sleeves of his blood-splattered, white uniform. Reaching toward the medicine shelf, he selected a chloroform tin. Using the same bottle of whiskey, one of the assistants in the room gave the feverish, moaning patient several swallows before he was silenced by a chloroform sponge and cone placed over his nose and mouth. After this was done, the doctor turned to work on another patient on another table in the crowded tent. The chloroform would take at least five minutes, or more, to induce sleep.

Elise felt nausea again in the back of her throat. She had never been around the sick and the wounded and the dying. Her thoughts flashed back to only a few weeks prior when she had attended the ball at the lovely Balfour House. She was young and happy and had danced for hours on end. Now, she felt old at the age of eighteen. So much had changed in only a few weeks' time. Her youth had fled. Would she ever marry and have children? She wondered whether she would even be alive if ever the war ended. For the first time in her life, she faced her own mortality. As usual, however, her thoughts quickly turned to Stone Jackson who embodied life, itself. She longed to see him again.

Her Aunt Celia was busy at another gurney in the tent. She was holding the hand of a young soldier and was trying to comfort him as he alternately screamed and cursed and cried. Elise saw something familiar about the boy and quickly realized that he was the young soldier who sat by her brother, Jack, on their train trip to Vicksburg. The dirty sheet which covered his body was soaked with blood from his knees to his feet. Another amputation, she thought, shuddering at the thought of it.

A few more minutes passed before the surgeon returned to the table where his patient had received chloroform. He had to work quickly, before the soldier could feel the pain of the amputation. With precision, the surgeon tied a tight cord around the mangled leg, then calling for a large knife, he cut through flesh and muscle down to the bone. Next, calling for a saw, he quickly removed the leg from the knee to the foot. The severed leg was thrown on the ground, which was littered with other limbs, hands, fingers and body parts. The stench in the tent was overpowering and sickening. After tying the artery with a small cord, he turned the flap of skin down over the stump and completed the amputation with stitches.

Elise felt herself growing weak, and the room seemed to be spinning around. Ashamed of her weakness, she held to the side of a table and found herself praying for strength…she who rarely prayed. "Help me to be strong, Lord," she prayed. She was thankful when her strength returned and she heard the doctor speaking to her.

"Laudanum, young lady…bring me some laudanum. Also, there's an amber-colored drip bottle of chloroform somewhere. See if you can find it for me."

Elise looked at the scant assortment of medicines on the narrow shelf, but she couldn't find the chloroform drip bottle. However, she saw a reddish-looking medicine with the label of laudanum, which her aunt had brought with her. She noticed the word "Poison" on the label of the transparent bottle. The doctor opened this and administered a dosage to the amputee, to deaden his pain when he became fully awake.

"Next!" the surgeon barked, as the table he had worked on was quickly replaced by the gurney with the young boy on it. Her aunt continued to hold the delirious boy's hand, as the surgeon removed the bloody sheet to inspect the horrific wound.

"I need more chloroform and laudanum,' he said in a tired voice. Elise found the medicines and handed the tin of chloroform to the surgeon. Holding the knife between his teeth, the surgeon soaked the sponge with chloroform and mechanically placed the sponge and cone over the soldier's mouth and nose. Everyone in the tent reeled from the smells and screams of the victims of combat.

Coughing and nauseated, Elise left the tent, along with several others, and breathed deeply into the fresh air and sunshine.

She looked back in the tent and could see her aunt still holding the hand of the nearly comatose boy as the surgeon prepared his leg amputation. Her cough and nausea better, she hurried back inside the tent. Finding a bucket of water, she filled a nearby cup and drank from it. Remembering the horses outside, she dipped some of the water into a smaller pail which she carried to the geldings. Since the sun had shifted, she moved them to the shadow of one of the tents, where she let them drink their fill of water.

Returning to the surgeon's tent, she tried to help others who were suffering. On one cot lay a soldier whose hair, eyelashes and eyebrows were singed from his head. His whole face was blackened and seared to a crisp with powder. When he moaned for water, Elise found another cup and dipped it into the water bucket. With the help of a nurse, they gently lifted the man's head and he feebly managed to drink some water.

Another soldier was being brought into the tent, and Elise heard one of the doctors exclaiming that the man had erysipelas. He appeared to be covered with red sores and had fever and chills. Several nurses washed their hands in chlorinated soda before following a doctor to the litter where the young soldier lay. Elise heard the doctor call for bromine-soaked dressing before sending the patient to another tent where he would be isolated from the other patients.

On the next table, Elise saw a large soldier who was wounded by a Minie ball passing through his heaving chest. His heart was palpitating to the extent that his whole body shook. On another gurney lay a soldier who had been shot through the jaw. His mouth was open and his tongue pulled back. Yet another soldier lay nearby with his head scalped. His jaws were locked, and he died with convulsions, as Elise was trying to think of a way to help him. With tears in her eyes, she moved on to other tables and litters, witnessing the cruelty and horrors of war.

Finding a horsehair fly whisk, she set about fanning the patients where flies swarmed around their wounds. She was moved to tears again when several of the patients, rendered inhuman by their injuries, thanked her in voices so low and ragged, she strained to hear them. Mosquitoes vied with flies under the hot tent, swarming around the wounded, then lighting on their festering injuries.

After hours of tending the sick and wounded, Elise noticed her aunt holding on to one of the beds, as she brushed at flies and mosquitoes which hovered over the patients. Elise immediately realized that her aunt had reached the limit of her endurance. It was time for them to go. She wondered when the surgeons and nurses would end their day, but something told her that they worked around the clock, grabbing a few hours rest when another shift relieved them.

Elise walked over to her aunt and put her arm around her shoulders. Her aunt's breathing was shallow and quick. She had reached the point of exhaustion. The thought went through Elise's mind that her Aunt Celia had finally realized that Vicksburg, after all, might become the key in Lincoln's pocket.

"Let's go home, Aunt Celia. You need to rest," Elise said. Her aunt who had always been so strong was now childlike and obedient. It frightened Elise when she realized that her aunt reminded her of their recently defeated army. She, also, was overcome and dejected.

"I'll drive," Elise said as she helped her aunt to the passenger's seat of the carriage, where she also climbed up to sit beside her. The carriage ride back to her aunt's house was uneventful, and Elise felt more comfortable managing the large horses. However, upon arriving back at the house, she was glad to see Sip who tended to the horses and carriage.

The church bells sounded in the early morning light of the

city which was now encircled by the enemy. It was a reminder to the faithful that it was Sunday morning and the rector of Christ Church had a message for his parishioners, if they were brave enough to make the trip from their homes and caves to the church. However, the constant cannonading from the enemy up the river was a reminder of what awaited the person who dared to walk out in the open.

Elise awakened to the sweet peals of the church chimes and suddenly felt a strong urge to go to church. She could not remember ever feeling such a need. Hurriedly, she dressed and went downstairs. She was surprised to see her aunt up and about and dressed for the day.

"Elise," I keep hearing the church bells, and I'm wondering whether we could attend the church service this morning. Alan said we'd probably be safer now to walk, rather than take the carriage. The potholes in the streets are so bad now, the horses could break their legs, and the carriages are not holding up well on the streets, either."

"Oh, Aunt Celia, I want to go, also. I waked up this morning, wanting to go."

"You need to eat something, Elise. I made a cup of our Confederate coffee. I'll make you a cup, if you want me to."

"No, that will take too long, and we need to go while the shelling is not as bad as it will be later. Actually, I'm not hungry. I'll leave Mama a note, telling her we are going to church." Celia found some paper for a note which Elise left on the table for her mother to read when she awakened.

"Lord, be with us and keep us safe," Celia Holmes said, bowing her head. Elise bowed her head, also, when she realized her aunt was praying. After this, they both put on their bonnets and began the long walk to the church.

The shelling was even louder outside the cave, and both

clung to each other as they made the walk into town. They were shocked at the appearance of the streets in the town. Large sinkholes made the streets almost impassable, the results of the heavy bombs lobbed from the enemy on the river below. Shells were everywhere, and some of the huge bombs lay unexploded along the streets where Elise and her aunt hurried with their heads down and with Celia Holmes holding onto Elise's arm. Many of the trees which had survived the shelling were shorn of their branches and leaves and were mere poles which dotted the in-town landscape.

They hurried by a man who was engrossed in licking something from the palm of his hand. Elise stared at the substance in his hand and was surprised to see raw sugar. Her aunt commented that people were paying enormous prices for sugar. Elise could not imagine how someone could eat just sugar, but she reasoned that a hungry person could eat just about anything.

Horses, standing on their hind legs and straining on their leashes, reached up for the few mulberry leaves on other trees near the officers' tents. Elise looked beyond the Rebel entrenchments and was shocked to see what looked like hundreds of swollen bodies of horses and mules which had necessarily been dumped into the river. Feeling nauseated at the sight, especially knowing that the troops relied on the river water for drinking and cooking, she hurried her aunt on to the church.

The missiles never let up in their quest to bring the town to total destruction and submission. As Elise and her aunt were nearing the church, they saw an orderly holding the reins of an officer's horse on the main street of the town. Elise was noting the erect bearing of the orderly when a noiseless cannonball, fired from nearby, struck the orderly's head and left him headless, but still holding the reins of the horse as if he were still alive.

Because of the quiet missile, the horse continued to stand

still, as did the headless corpse. Elise and her aunt gasped at the scene, as men on the street rushed to the victim, causing the horse to rear up in fright and the body to fall to the street. Elise screamed as her aunt cried out, sobbing and holding onto her, almost causing both of them to fall. Feeling her legs beginning to buckle, Elise lowered her head and held onto her aunt as they neared the church grounds which were strewn with shells and debris. Though the adjacent rectory had been damaged by the soaring missiles, the church's ivy-clad tower remained untouched.

Upon entering the church, they found it filled with a congregation of bloodstained and powder-grimed soldiers. They were sitting on pews covered with mortar, bricks and glass. The rubble from the constant shelling was so deep on the pews that Elise and her Aunt Celia didn't try to remove it. Rather, they sat on top of it, hoping the glass shards wouldn't cut through their clothes.

Other civilians had braved the airborne missiles to attend the service, so the room was nearly full of worshipers, some of whom had slept on the pews during the night. The Reverend W.W. Lord welcomed his parishioners with a smile, observing their sad and worried faces. He then told them about a rather humorous event that had happened to him one evening, as he was returning home from church. He happened upon a large, burly man riding in his wagon, when suddenly the man jumped down from his wagon and crawled under it. As the puzzled priest watched him, the man would peep out one side of the wagon, then the other, looking up into the air above him. Finally, after a full minute of dodging back and forth, the wagoner ducked out to see what the supposed weapon above him was going to do.

"Looking over at me," the rector said, "he grunted, 'Why don't it bust?' Well, for a full minute, he had been playing hide and seek with one of our lightning bugs...or fireflies!" This brought smiles and even some hearty laughs from those in the congregation.

The priest then opened his Bible to several texts which he shared with the faithful. Elise found a Bible and opened it to Psalm 27 and followed the words as the rector read them out loud.

"The Lord is my light and my salvation; whom shall I fear? The Lord is the strength of my life; of whom shall I be afraid?

"When the wicked, even mine enemies and my foes, came upon me to eat up my flesh, they stumbled and fell.

"Though an host should encamp against me, my heart shall not fear: though war should rise against me, in this will I be confident.

"One thing have I desired of the Lord, that will I seek after; that I may dwell in the house of the Lord all the days of my life, to behold the beauty of the Lord, and to enquire in his temple.

"For in the time of trouble he shall hide me in his pavilion: in the secret of his tabernacle shall he hide me; he shall set me up upon a rock.

"And now shall mine head be lifted up above mine enemies round about me: therefore, will I offer in his tabernacle sacrifices of joy; I will sing, yea, I will sing praises unto the Lord.

"Hear, O Lord, when I cry with my voice: have mercy also upon me, and answer me.

"When thou saidst, Seek ye my face; my heart said unto thee, Thy face, Lord, will I seek.

"Hide not thy face far from me; put not thy servant away in anger: thou hast been my help; leave me not, neither forsake me, O God of my salvation.

"When my father and my mother forsake me, then the Lord will take me up.

"Teach me thy way, O Lord, and lead me in a plain path, because of mine enemies.

"Deliver me not over unto the will of mine enemies: for false witnesses are risen up against me, and such as breathe out cruelty.

"I had fainted, unless I had believed to see the goodness of the Lord in the land of the living.

"Wait on the Lord: be of good courage, and he shall strengthen thine heart: wait, I say, on the Lord."

Closing the Bible, Elise felt some consolation from the words. The pastor enlarged upon their meaning, speaking of David who lived several thousand years before. David, too, was surrounded by those who would kill him, but he called on the Lord who protected him. Today, on behalf of all of his congregation, the Reverend Lord called on the Lord to keep all of them safe. The gentle, kind words of the pastor brought some peace to Elise's heart, something she desperately needed.

Chapter Four

Several days lapsed before Jack brought Elise word, on a late afternoon, that Grant's army was beginning a siege of the city. Their Uncle Alan, he said, told him to tell them to go to the cellar of Christ Church where others in the town were planning to gather. Christ Church was built of stone and brick and was probably the safest place to stay at that time. They should use their cave later, he said, because it needed more work done inside it.

Elise couldn't help but notice that her brother's uniform, once so crisp and clean, was now dirty and torn. It had taken on the butternut hue of other rumpled Confederate uniforms, and she guessed he had worn the same uniform for weeks now. There were none others to spare. Though she and Jack had always had the typical fusses and childish squabbles, growing up, now she sensed a tenderness for him, which she had heretofore never felt. As he left, shutting the door behind him, she felt tears stinging her eyes.

Elise gathered her mother and aunt and the two black servants and they began walking to Christ Church. The shells were now being shot from the land forces on the East of the town, along with the naval force on the river to the West, below the town. Looking up at the sky, she saw the small, hydrogen-filled balloons which she had heard about, floating over the city. They bore leaflets from the Federals, aimed at undermining the will of the people to support the Confederate cause. Elise began praying each step of the way. Upon entering the church, which was filled with shards of bricks, mortar, and glass, they walked down the steps to the cellar, where some people had already gathered.

The dank cellar was lit by the fitful glow of three tallow candles. A coal-heap covered with rugs and blankets provided sitting space for Elise and her mother and aunt. Chloee and Sip found another pile of coal, also covered with rugs and blankets, where they sat.

When the booms of the Union's guns sounded, the candles flickered and the church shook. As the hours wore on, everyone in the gloomy cellar tried to find space enough to sleep through the night, but their sleep was fitful, disturbed not only by the shells of the enemy but also by the realization that the war was escalating and they wondered whether they would live through it.

The next morning, Alan Holmes appeared in the cellar. Looking disheveled and worried, he urged them to run to their cave, as quickly as possible, and to stay there day and night. There wasn't time now for the cave to be enlarged. Grant's army was only a mile or so away from the eastern side of Vicksburg, he said. The enemy's shots and cannon were now being fired to the eastern part of the city, while their navy fleet on the Mississippi River kept up its bombardment of the town from the West. No one was safe. The cave was their only hope to provide some protection. After a quick hug to his wife and a nod to Elise and Abby, Alan Holmes left as quickly as he had come.

Elise wondered how she and the others could run to the cave. Her mother and aunt were like children now. Her Aunt Celia, once the high-spirited lady she had always loved and admired was now fearful and heavyhearted. She and her mother, Abby, both had tears in their eyes, and Elise had to insist that they leave the church and follow her. Sip and Chloee, still crouching on a coal bin, told Elise they would follow later. Their eyes were large with fright, and Elise didn't know what to do, other than let them stay there.

Others who had stayed overnight in the church cellar heeded Alan Holmes' advice, also. They quickly left the cellar and began running toward their homes and caves. Elise shepherded her mother and aunt out of the church and urged them toward their cave. The thunder of artillery from the enemy across the river, and now behind them on the eastern side of the city, was deafening and frightening. She knew they were desperately dodging these shells as they whizzed by them, wreaking havoc in the city.

Walking in the middle, Elise had an arm around her mother and the other arm around her aunt. The cave was several blocks away, and she prayed they would arrive there alive. As she struggled to reach their cave, she felt a mighty jolt, as her mother screamed and slumped from her arm to the ground. Blood was seeping into her clothing, and she was alternately screaming and begging for help.

Elise saw an ambulance in the distance and began waving her arms for it to stop. The open, bullet-ridden conveyance with large wooden wheels, pulled by two horses, halted beside them, its driver and helper jumping to the ground. With her mother weeping and attempting to hold on to her, Elise watched as the men in white, bloodstained coats, lifted her mother and placed her on a gurney in the ambulance. They then quickly asked Elise where she was going.

"We were told to go to our cave and to stay there," she said, her voice trembling.

"Well, get in the ambulance," the driver said, "and we'll carry you to your cave after we leave the hospital."

"Oh, thank you!" Elise said with tears in her eyes. The men helped her and her aunt into the now crowded ambulance and then proceeded to the nearest hospital with its siren wailing. At the hospital, they took her mother from the ambulance, as Elise and her Aunt Celia said their goodbyes.

"I'll come to see about you, Mama," Elise said, adding, "We love you."

"You stay safe," her mother replied in a voice coarsened with pain and tears.

"This is the Duff-Green House," Celia Holmes said softly in a quavering voice, as the orderlies rolled Abby Holmes into the makeshift hospital. "It's a hospital now, and I hear the northern prisoners are kept on the top floor, so the boats on the river will avoid shelling the house." As if in denial of what her aunt said, the Parrott shells and Minie balls still flew around them, causing the horses to snort and rear up with fright, as the ambulance driver and his helper climbed back into the ambulance.

"We've got 6,000 in our hospitals now," the driver volunteered before hastily asking about directions to the Holmes' cave. After quickly giving directions to their cave, Elise remembered her fears of living in the cave and realized that she was now grateful for such a shelter away from the barrage of missiles destroying the town.

As the ambulance entered the ledge in front of their dugout, Elise saw that things had changed since her initial visit to their cave several weeks before. Now, it seemed that everyone was in their caves. Some people were outside their dugouts, attempting to find rocks and tinder for their fire pits, for cooking, which they planned to build just outside the open entrances of their caves, as the shells continued to streak over them.

After thanking the ambulance driver and his assistant, Elise was now the one to lead her aunt into the dark recesses of the cave. Upon entering the cave, she could hear voices from the caves which led into theirs. She could hear children crying and could hear mingled voices from both of the caves which adjoined her aunt's dugout.

She remembered the lamp near the entrance of the cave, but she didn't have a match to light it. She fumbled around on the damp floor of the cave until she felt a matchbox. After lighting the lamp, she looked closely at her aunt who appeared to be dazed and who had not said a word.

"Aunt Celia, you probably need to go to your room and rest," Elise said as she picked up the lamp and guided her aunt inside the cave.

"Is it safe?" her aunt stammered in a weak voice.

"Aunt Celia, it's safer than being outside," Elise said, drawing the sheet curtain aside for her aunt to enter the room which she and her uncle had paid to be hollowed out of the hillside. Tears filled Elise's eyes as her aunt crept over to one of the narrow cots in the room and lay down on it. Adjusting a pillow under her aunt's head, Elise found some sheets and quilts which were folded on the other cot and spread a sheet over her.

As Elise left the room, she looked back and realized that her aunt was sound asleep. She's exhausted, Elise thought, finding it difficult to accept the different person her beloved aunt had become since the war had escalated.

Tired and frightened, Elise remembered her aunt asking Sip and Chloee to carry water to their cave, but upon looking in each room of the cave, she found no water. Had someone stolen the water or had Sip and Chloee just neglected to bring any to the cave? She didn't know, but she did know that she had to go up the hill behind the cave to her aunt's house and fill the bucket in the house with water from the cistern. How thankful she was for the clean water in the cistern on the back porch…and that it was free! She knew that others were buying water by the bucketful. With these thoughts running through her mind, she knew she had to hurry before her aunt awakened, upset to find her gone.

The cannonading of enemy shells had slowed somewhat, as she began climbing the hill behind the cave. Her long homespun dress kept tripping her, slowing any progress in her ascent. The cows in the open rail fence behind the house eyed her as she finally reached level ground behind the large house. One began moving toward her as she held up her dress and fled into the house. She knew the cows were hungry, but she had nothing to feed them. She knew they could drink water from any of the several streams which flowed through the grounds of her aunt's home. She was amazed but thankful that the cows were still alive after the enemy's bombardment.

Vaguely, she wondered where Coco, the mule, was, also the Percherons which had necessarily been turned out of the stable to graze. She felt they had either wandered out of the open gate, or the Yankees had possibly stolen them. No one had been able to feed them, so maybe they were being fed by the Yanks. She wondered whether her uncle knew. She guessed that he had had no choice but to let the mule and the carriage horses graze on their own.

Elise walked through the house, looking for a bucket to fill with water. Finding the bucket which was heavy, she wondered how she could carry it filled with water back to the cave. As she began looking for a pail to dip the water from the cistern on the back porch, she heard a noise at the front door and then a man's voice. Frightened, she wondered whether the man might be a Yankee, for she remembered the soldiers who had taken her aunt's chickens. The man spoke again, and his voice was strangely familiar. Elise ran to the parlor and into the arms of Stone Jackson. "Whoa, young lady," Stone said, holding her by the shoulders.

Elise was so happy to see him that she threw her arms around his neck and, without a word, laid her head on his chest. She couldn't speak…she just wanted to be held. The events of the day had left her exhausted and terrified.

"Elise, are you all right?" Stone asked, stroking her hair and kissing her cheeks. When she looked up at him, he kissed her mouth. Elise clung to him as he pulled her even closer. She dropped her head on his chest, still clinging to him. Finally, she was able to speak.

"I came for some water," she said, her voice trembling. Before he could answer, she hurriedly told him of being in the church cellar during the bombardment and of attempting to walk with her mother and aunt to their cave. She told him of her mother being wounded and about the ambulance which took her mother to the hospital and them to their cave. Stone continued to hold her until she had poured out her heart to him. Now, she told him, she had found a bucket and was going to take water back to their cave.

"You can't manage the bucket, Elise. What you need to do, before the shells begin flying again, is to get a few things here for you and your aunt and put them in a bag. Then, you can ride behind me on Blackberry. I'll take you to your cave and I'll come back and get some water for you. It would be too heavy for you to carry. By the way, where are your aunt's servants?"

"They wanted to stay at Christ Church," Elise said.

"Well, don't expect them to come back," Stone said, adding, "you know that Grant and Sherman, and probably by now 45,000 of their army, are only a mile or so from here. It would only be a short walk for the servants to join the northern army. They wouldn't have to float on a log across the river, as others have done in the past. Now, they can just walk over to Grant's army. No, I don't think you will see them again."

"I can't believe they would leave Uncle Alan and Aunt Celia," Elise said.

"They want to be free," Stone said, and Elise was puzzled by his answer. Hadn't her aunt and uncle always been good to their black servants? She found it hard to believe that they would just leave without even a goodbye. They had lived at Belle Voir as long as she could remember, and they always appeared to be happy there. The thought came to her that maybe they were after food.

There was precious little of that left in her aunt's house.

The house shook as a missile flew above it, causing something from the chimney above the fireplace to become dislodged and to drift downward. Suddenly, a chirping sound from the cold fireplace caused Elise and Stone to stare at the sparrow which was patiently picking up parts of its nest and reascending the chimney with the lost nesting material in its beak. This resiliency of nature in the midst of war never failed to strengthen Elise, for she marveled at the ability of the small creatures to go about their lives as if a future awaited them, after all.

As Elise was thinking about a response to Stone's words about her aunt's servants, they heard the shriek of another huge missile which became louder as it dropped from its arc in the sky to the ground by her aunt's home. It tore into the music room near the parlor where Stone had quickly pulled Elise into a far corner of the room, covering her on the floor with his body.

Looking at the gaping hole in the wall, they saw that the house was on fire. Stone quickly lifted Elise from the floor, at the same time asking where they could find towels or anything to soak in water to put out the fire. While Elise looked for towels, Stone found buckets which he quickly filled with water and proceeded to douse the flames which were gaining strength inside the house, edging closer to the large piano.

Elise soaked towels and other cloths in water and gave some to Stone. They slapped at the flames until Stone left to get more water. When he returned and threw more water on the weakened fire, they were thankful to have contained it. However, now the large, gaping hole in the wall had to be dealt with.

"Get me a sheet, Elise, and I'll hang it over the damaged area." When Elise returned with one of her aunt's bed linens, Stone had found a hammer and nails on the back porch, which he used to hang the sheet and cover the hole in the wall.

"Now, we need to salvage some wood from your aunt's rail fence, so I can make some temporary repairs outside. Let's see what we can find. I have something I want to show you, anyway, besides getting the wood."

"All right, let's go," Elise said, her voice trembling and her legs weak and unsteady, as she led the way to the back porch. Once outside, they walked around and looked at what was left of the huge bomb which remained by the outside wall of the music room in the crater it had made. It was still smoking but the fire was gone. She looked over into the pasture and did not see any of the cows. She guessed they probably left when the bomb hit her aunt's house.

Stone took Elise's hand and led her to the largest stream which flowed slowly through her aunt's property. Elise could remember playing in the water as a child when she visited her aunt and uncle during many summers. It was much as she remembered it, but now it appeared larger, more circular, and she saw some bubbles of activity in the water. It was a beaver with a large branch in its mouth, swimming toward the dam it was building. As she stood mesmerized by the swimming beaver which paid no attention to her and Stone, nor to the missiles flying overhead, she felt Stone's arm around her waist, pulling her to him.

As they stood there, spellbound by the labor of the beaver, Elise glanced behind the beaver which was patiently adding the branch in its mouth to the dam in progress. Another beaver, with several little beavers swimming alongside and behind her, also held a tree limb in her mouth.

The scene was so idyllic that Elise felt herself relax, even as the missiles streaked above them in the sky. Though she knew her aunt would not want the beavers cutting down the trees left on her acreage, the peaceful work of the beaver family brought a soothing calm, and for the moment the pastoral scene gave her peace. In spite of death and destruction all around, the beavers carried on with their lives as if they had hope for the future, something which she needed, also.

"I'm glad you brought me here, Stone," she said.

"I think we can take some lessons from these creatures. They are doing what beavers have done through the ages. They carry on and live their lives, like the sparrow in your aunt's chimney."

"It's calming to me, Stone. The rippling of the water and the little ones swimming around have a soothing effect that I haven't felt in a long time."

"Good," Stone said, again taking her by her hand. "Come on...I have something else to show you." Elise followed along beside him as they made their way to a nearby mulberry tree, shorn of most of its limbs by enemy bullets, but yet providing a place for a bird's nest on its lowest branch. As a Minie ball shrieked overhead, Elise looked into the nest and saw four blue eggs. Seeing the mother bluebird nearby, they both moved away from the nest.

"I'm pretty sure that's the mama bird, wanting to check on her eggs," he said as the bird flapped her wings and approached the nest.

Elise was overwhelmed with his gentleness and especially with his attempts to bring her calmness and serenity. For the first time since the war escalated, she felt protected and less fearful. Tears came to her eyes as she put her arms around his neck and rested her head on his chest. She felt the beating of his heart quicken as she snuggled against him. He held her until she spoke to him again, suggesting that they go back inside the house.

"All right...I left Blackberry out in front," he said, as he walked over to the rail fence and grabbed several of the long wood rails. These he laid at the back door.

"I'll just get some clothes for Aunt Celia and myself," she said, as she stepped up to the porch door.

"I'll wait on you while you get your clothes," Stone said, adding, "I have something in my haversack for you and your aunt, but now I'm going to need the hammer and nails again."

"All right, I won't be long," Elise said.

Elise hurried up the stairs to her room and gathered an armful of her clothing before going to her aunt's room downstairs. There, she picked up several homespun dresses and underclothing from the chifforobe in her aunt's bedroom. Finding a bag for the clothing, she joined Stone in the parlor where he was waiting, after nailing some boards outside over the large hole in the wall.

"Here is what I have for you and your Aunt Celia," Stone said, reaching in his haversack and handing Elise something wrapped in paper with a string around it. "It's salt mackerel," he said, adding, "It's been soaked and fried. There's a dearth of it in these parts, I hear. I'll keep it until we go back to the cave," he said, reaching for the packet and placing it again in his haversack.

"Oh, thank you so much, Stone! I don't know when we've had fish to eat!"

"You are welcome," he said as Elise reached up and kissed him, causing him to smile and to take her into his arms.

"Come, my dear Elise," Stone said, releasing her and picking up the bag of clothes before leading her by the hand outside, where Blackberry waited by the mounting block. Stone untied the horse, then using the stirrups he climbed into the saddle and shifted the bag of clothing to the front part of the saddle, along with his haversack. Reaching down for Elise who waited on the horse block, he quickly pulled her up to ride in the saddle behind him.

It was a tight squeeze with two in the saddle, but Elise refused to worry about the way she looked, with her dress drawn up to her knees on either side of the saddle and her bare legs pressed against a man she hardly knew, though she felt she had known him all of her life. She held on to Stone, with arms around his waist, as he guided the horse out of the driveway and back to the cave. When they reached the cave, Stone turned halfway in the saddle and lifted Elise to the ground.

"I'll be back in a little while with water," Stone said, handing her the bag of clothing and the packet of salt mackerel, as he shook the reins and headed back to her aunt's house.

Upon entering the dugout and finding her aunt still asleep, Elise put the food packet on a nearby table and the bag of clothing on the settee before sitting down in one of the chairs in the cave and awaiting Stone's return. She wondered how her aunt could continue to sleep with so much noise from the other inhabitants of the adjoining caves. Her heart was full of all that had happened during the day.

She remembered Stone's arms around her and the feel of his mouth on hers. She remembered the feeling of safety as he held her with his heartbeat so close to hers. What was the meaning of it all? What was the meaning of anything anymore?

Only a few weeks before, everything had held promise. She had heard that General Johnston was on his way with 50,000 men to join those at Vicksburg. What had happened to him and his army? Everyone had said that Vicksburg would never be taken. Why, only a few weeks ago, they had attended the ball at the lovely Balfour home, and everyone was laughing and having fun. She had felt young and beautiful in the dress from Madame Cognaisse's shop.

Now, everything had changed. She looked down at her homespun dress which had dirt on it from her climb up the embankment above their cave to her aunt's house. The dress was loose on her now. She knew she had lost weight, along with everyone else and with all of the animals in town. No one, and nothing, had enough food to eat now. As she sat, she closed her eyes and realized that she was praying again. She felt as if she had almost lived a long lifetime. She wondered whether she looked as old as she was beginning to feel now.

Hearing a noise at the entrance of the cave, she met Stone as he brought the filled bucket and a kettle full of water from the cistern in her aunt's house. He asked where to put them, and she pulled aside the improvised curtain to one of the empty rooms and asked him to put them there. Next, he quickly returned to the mouth of the cave and looked out.

"Come here, Elise, I want to show you something," he said. Elise followed him out of the cave, wondering what he was about to show her. He was looking toward the opposite hill where a large cow was grazing on its side. Elise wondered where the cow had come from, since all beef cattle had disappeared from the town since shortly after the siege began.

The cow appeared to be oblivious to the danger of the shelling which tore up the turf of the hill where it grazed. Rather, it ascended higher and higher until it reached the 200-foot crest of the ridge. That's when a hail of bullets from the Federal army sent it tumbling down the hill, its hooves clawing the air and mortally wounded, to the valley below. Without considering her own struggle with not having enough to eat, Elise felt terrible about the fate of the poor cow. Would she and others meet its fate, also? Before she could comment on all she had witnessed, Stone was telling her a quick goodbye as they walked back into the cave. He said he would get some of the meat and would bring it back to them. As he turned to leave, Celia Holmes appeared, pulling back the curtain of her bedroom in the cave.

"Welcome to our cave, Stone," she said with a smile.

"Thank you, Mrs. Holmes," Stone said.

"Stone brought us some salt mackerel," Elise said. "I told him we hadn't eaten fish in a long while. He also brought us some water, Aunt Celia."

"I remember asking Sip and Chloee to bring water to the cave, but they didn't do it. Thank you so much for bringing the water and the salt mackerel. Thank you for helping us!" she exclaimed with tears in her eyes.

"I told Elise I will help you in any way I can. She told me your servants wanted to stay at Christ Church when you left there earlier. I doubt they will be back, Mrs. Holmes. I know that many servants have left to go over to the northern side, and more are leaving every day. They can just walk a mile or so now and meet up with Grant's army where they'll get food and freedom. Don't expect them back."

"Well, I just can't imagine their leaving us, when we need them now more than ever."

"They may find, later on, that freedom isn't what they thought it would be, but for now, they're hungry and scared. They won't be back."

"Stone, how can we repay you for all you are doing for us?"

"I don't want or expect any pay…I just want to see Elise as often as I can get away and come here. If I can help her or you or any of your family, please let me know."

Celia Holmes dabbed at her eyes and thanked him, adding that she certainly approved of Stone's coming to see Elise as often as he wanted to. After thanking him again for the fish and for his help, she told Elise that she was leaving to visit with Isabel Davis for a little while, since the shelling had lessened.

"Please be careful, Aunt Celia. Also, we need to tell Mrs. Isabel and Drusie about the meetings which we want to have in your cave. You were the one who suggested that we do that."

"You're right…I'll tell them. We probably need to meet soon," she said as she waved goodbye and left the cave. As Stone turned to leave, he told Elise that he was going to carry her mother some mackerel which he had kept for her in his haversack. Elise thanked him again for his thoughtfulness.

"Elise, this is the last time I can ride Blackberry here," Stone said. "We've gotten word that the shelling is going to increase a hundredfold. Grant and his army are only a little over a mile from here now. I will walk here and check on you as often as I can. Also, I want you to know that we're having to send our mules over to the other side. We can't feed them and they're skin and bones. You will probably hear them as they're driven down Jackson Street over to the Yanks. They plan to send over 700 mules in the morning and 900 more tomorrow evening."

Stunned, Elise didn't know what to say. She remembered noticing the thin animals when she first arrived in Vicksburg. She had wondered then whether Vicksburg was losing the battle. Stone walked over to Elise and wrapped his arms around her.

"I love you, Elise," he whispered, giving her a kiss on her upturned lips. "I know, any other time, your family would think I'm too old for you, and we've only known each other a short while. However, I feel that I've known you all of my life. I realize you are young and innocent, and I don't want to do anything to destroy that, for it's only one of the many things that I love about you."

"I don't feel young and innocent anymore, Stone. I've witnessed amputations and I've seen my mother struck by enemy shells. I've grown old fast, Stone."

"You are beautiful, Elise," he said, looking her over from head to toe. "Do you love me, Elise?" he asked, holding her away from him and looking into her eyes.

"How could I not love you?" Elise said, going back into his arms and cupping his face with her hands. "You are my strength," she said, trying hard not to shed any tears, and adding softly, "…you and the Lord."

She laid her head on his chest and silently thanked God for the raw power that emanated from this man who provided a shelter in the storm of war. What would she do without him, she wondered, as he tenderly stroked her hair and face? She knew that she could rest forever in his arms.

Chapter Five

Elise's first night in the cave passed by uneventfully, though shells from the enemy awakened her during the night, making the cave shake. The next morning, she heard hundreds of animal hooves pounding the dirt, and she realized that what Stone had told her about the Confederate mules was coming to pass. She hurriedly pulled on her stockings and shoes, then fled to the mouth of the cave and looked toward Jackson Street where she could see plumes of dust rising in the sky, midst the sounds of hooves and shouting men. She wondered whether the animals would find enough food on the Yankees' side to survive.

Others stood outside their caves, also, looking toward the sounds of the mass exodus of mules, then looking at one another, as if for answers. Elise spoke to her nearest cave neighbors, telling them what she had been told about the starving mules. She told them that 700 were to be driven over that morning and 900 more that evening. She saw the tears in the eyes of those closest to her and the looks of hopelessness on their faces.

When Elise reentered the cave, she met the older man and his wife whose dugout was connected to theirs. They asked permission to use some of the empty rooms of her aunt's cave, as some of their relatives and friends had not had time to dig their own caves and needed a place to stay. Since her aunt was still asleep, Elise immediately gave them permission, knowing her aunt would want to help them. She also felt that she and her aunt could share the front room, since her mother was in the hospital.

Elise noticed a young couple with an infant taking one of

the rooms, along with several black servants who took another room. A third room was taken by a man and his wife, named Mr. and Mrs. Wilson. The man's leg had recently been amputated and as he hobbled into the room, Elise was reminded of her father, and her eyes filled with tears. Their new tenants asked permission to use the water they found, which Stone had left in one of the rooms, and when Elise told them they could, they immediately cupped their hands and drank from the bucket and kettle which Stone had filled.

    Late that evening, as Stone had told her, Elise once again heard the sound of the mules being driven over to the Yankees' side, since they were starving in the town. She remembered that Stone had said that 900 mules would be driven over in the evening.

    She had heard that the bodies of horses and mules were being dumped by the bluecoats into the Yazoo River just above Vicksburg. She guessed that these were animals which had been hit by Rebel fire. She also knew that water from the river below the Yazoo was brought up in large tankards for the Rebel army, and she wondered whether this filthy water was why so many of their soldiers were sick in the hospitals. Her Uncle Alan instructed Jack to drink water from the cistern on his back porch, but sometimes it wasn't possible for him to walk to the cistern. His uncle always urged him to ride his own horse there to get water.

    Elise finally found a time when no one was around to tell her Aunt Celia about the bomb which destroyed the outside wall of her music room. Her reaction to hearing about the bomb hitting her house was for Elise to thank Stone Jackson for patching up the wall of the music room. Her aunt didn't seem interested in going back to her house to look at the damage. She was fearful of even stepping outside their cave. Maybe after the war was over, she said, she and Alan could repair their home. She also was glad that the people could use the unoccupied rooms of her cave, agreeing that she and

Elise could share the front room of the dugout.

Elise awakened early the next morning to the terrified anxiety of other denizens in surrounding caves, involving one of the largest caves on a high hill in Vicksburg. The cave was not far from the pickets of the notorious northern General William Tecumseh Sherman. It seemed that two hundred people were sleeping on planks, laid along the floor of the large cave. Mortars from the Feds across the river were sending their shells hot and heavy, when one buried itself some six feet into the earth above the cave and exploded. This dislocated dirt in the cave, which buried a young child beneath it. Some of the men in the cave pulled the little girl from under the mass of dirt and rubble. Though blood was gushing from her eyes and nose and ears and mouth, initially, she was later thought to be recovering.

As Elise heard this terrible news from a passing courier, neighbors in the dugouts near the Holmes' cave began gathering in the cave and found seats in the large middle room of the dugout. Everyone felt the need of comfort from one another midst the constant shelling and also the desire for any news that any of them might have. Elise lit candles in the room to dispel the oppressive early-morning darkness.

"Lord a'mercy! I heard that a baby was born in the back of that cave at the same time the child was buried," one of the mothers present said. Hearing this, all of the mothers in the cave quickly glanced at Sybil Adams who was obviously expecting another child. She sat with her two young daughters at the rear of the Holmes' cave. They all smiled at her in recognition of all she was experiencing in trying to keep her children and herself alive and well. Different ones in the caves had been sharing what little food they had with her since the siege began. After several moments of silence, the occupants of the caves began telling what news they had of the war.

"I heard some terrible news yesterday," an old man in the room said. "In one of our hospitals, some of our soldiers had undergone operations, when a shell exploded and six men had to have limbs amputated. Some who had already had a leg taken off at the ankle had to have the leg taken off to the thigh. One who had lost one arm had to have the other one taken off. Sometimes, I wonder whether what our boys are fighting for is worth it!"

Isabel Davis spoke up and said her husband had sent an orderly to tell her what happened at the City Hospital. It seemed that two doctors were catching up on some sleep in the wee hours of the morning when a 15-inch mortar struck the hospital. It destroyed everything in its path, including the upper stories, walls, and ceilings.

"You know," she said, "the City Hospital stands on what some say is the highest ground in Vicksburg and is a continuous target for heavy shells from Porter's mortar boats three miles away, as the crow flies. Well, the shell exploded in the room where the surgeons were asleep. One doctor managed to leave the room, but the other one was covered with a load of plastering and debris. The shell, he said, exploded with a deafening noise, filling the room with hundreds of broken fragments and flames and suffocating smoke. The doctor lost a leg and had his lung pierced. His knee also was injured. He knew he was bleeding to death, so he extricated himself from the debris and had presence of mind enough to tie his arteries to stop the bleeding. I tell you, our hospitals are the most dangerous places to be. Eight were killed and fourteen were wounded. The orderly said Porter's missiles looked like big potash kettles until they burst. Then, they exploded like aerial powder magazines."

As everyone in the cave looked at one another with terror written across their faces, Jack suddenly appeared in the doorway of the cave with another young man. All eyes were riveted first on

Jack, then on the other person who appeared to have been doused in the nearby river. Both were out of breath, apparently having been running to avoid the constant shelling that exploded all around them. Jack finally caught his breath after nodding to Elise and his Aunt Celia before addressing the group.

"I want you all to hear from one of our couriers who just came up from the river," he said. "He doesn't want his name given, but I can tell you how he received the information he's about to give you. He brought some messages from General Johnston, which he has already given to General Pemberton. To bring these messages to us, he had to float on a log down the Yazoo and Mississippi rivers, through enemy territory, braving alligators and possibly malaria in the swamps. You know, everyone calls the Yazoo the river of death now. He's a hero to me," Jack said, shaking the wet hand of the courier.

The courier nodded his head, first to Jack, then to the group sitting in the candlelight of the cave. His hair was plastered to his head from having to duck underwater when he passed by enemy boats in the rivers. His clothes were still drenched, leaving drops on the floor of the cave, as he addressed the group.

"Thank you, Jack. I made a copy of General Johnston's message to General Pemberton, so I could share it with you and others," the courier said as he reached inside his wet shirt pocket for the handwritten copy he had made and proceeded to relate what he had managed to bring to them.

"Near the end of May, General Pemberton got dispatches from General Johnston that he was at Canton with a large force, and Loring was at Jackson with ten thousand men. He also read that General Bragg's army was coming from Tennessee to assist Johnston, so relief was on the way. It was reported from the East that General Lee had driven Hooker over the Potomac with the Federals losing eighty thousand men. He heard that Long Bridge had been burned and Arlington Heights was held by the Virginians.

"Then, he heard over the grapevine telegraph that Price was in control of Helena, Arkansas, and also the Mississippi, that Bragg was occupying Memphis, thereby closing Grant's communication with the North. He also received messages that Lee was shelling Washington City from Arlington Heights and that Kirby Smith was at New Carthage, Louisiana. He was informed that Semmes with a strong fleet of iron-clad boats had routed Farragut and recaptured New Orleans and was moving up the river with Magruder and Dick Taylor to capture Banks and his army and to finish off Grant and Porter."

As everyone sat, rapt and wide-eyed, the courier continued, "General Pemberton keeps getting word of Johnston's advance. He keeps hearing that Johnston has crossed the Big Black River and has demolished Grant's wagon train. We hope we can expect him here soon!"

As the courier concluded his mission and looked around the dugout, everyone began clapping and several of the men in the room let out the bloodcurdling Rebel war cry, followed by more clapping. Waving goodbye to Elise and his Aunt Celia, Jack and the courier left as quickly as they had arrived. Everyone in the cave was cheered by the courier's news, and the meeting was quickly adjourned. Families began moving back to their own caves.

Days went by, with the cave dwellers trying to survive the constant bombardment of the cone-shaped Parrott shells and the whistling Minie balls. Dogs which belonged to the people in the caves were maddened by the noise of the shells, darting down the ledges in front of the caves, howling and barking. Stray dogs roamed around the dugouts, looking for food, then cowered in the caves when shells burst near them. People in the caves were fearful of them, afraid that they might assault them in their hunger. Others were used as food for the starving citizenry.

Several times, Jack appeared at their cave with news from the trenches. General Johnston was expected soon, he said. General Pemberton had received word that General Johnston was at Yazoo city, less than fifty miles away. Everyone was heartened by the prospect of his arrival with thousands of men to help in the defense of Vicksburg.

Elise quickly learned that the only safe times to go into town were around 8:00 o'clock in the mornings, at noon, and at 8:00 o'clock in the evenings. She guessed that these were times when the enemy soldiers were eating and letting their guns cool, and when they took a break from shelling the town. She hadn't yet made the long walk into town, as Jack and her Uncle Alan had tried to supply her and her Aunt Celia with food from the market place. The food became scarcer as the siege progressed, and Elise heard that only mule meat and rat meat were now available at the downtown market. She knew it was becoming more difficult for both her brother and her uncle to make the trip to the market and the cave, as they were needed more than ever now in the trenches.

Now that Grant's troops formed a half circle around the east side of Vicksburg, the fighting became even more vicious and intense. The Northern dead fell where they were hit in the ravines and on top of the embankments between the caves on the east of the city and the surrounding Union army, only about a mile or so away from the caves, also east of the city. After three days in the sun, the stench of decomposing bodies drifted across the hills and into the caves.

On an early morning, Elise awakened to the usual odors of unwashed bodies and full chamber pots, but the added smell of rotting corpses made her nauseous. However, the tweeting of birds as they flew about and gathered materials for the nests they were building helped her spirits. Always, these pleasant sounds of the routines of nature never failed to bring some semblance of peace in her heart. How many of the mother birds' nests had been destroyed by the constant pounding of enemy shells, she wondered, as she crawled from her makeshift bed in the cave.

She could hear snores and babies crying from other residents of the caves, as she made an attempt to brush her hair and wash her face with the little amount of water which was left in her room in the cave. She planned to make the long trip to the market place for food and to visit her mother at the Duff-Green House, which was now a hospital.

Elise had heard from an orderly, sent by her Uncle Alan, that a three-hour truce had been agreed upon between Grant and Pemberton, since the wounded and dead bluecoats were causing a stench around the city, as they lay on the ground between the two battle sites. Since their supply of water was low, she decided to climb the hill above their cave and maybe take a much-needed bath from the cistern on the back porch of her aunt's home. She could also bring some water back with her. Since her aunt was still sleeping, she decided not to wake her. Instead, she set out with several light jugs for the water she would bring back.

As she began the climb up the hill, she could see over into the pasture where the farm animals usually stayed, though the gate remained open. However, as she climbed, she did not see any of the animals. CoCo, the mule, was still gone, also. She wondered whether he had been herded along with the 1600 which had been driven over to Grant's side weeks before. She had noticed the poor animal becoming thinner and thinner, so she hoped he had found food on the other side. Something told her that someone should look in the coach house to check on the carriage, since the Percherons were gone. How could it be stolen? She thought it would be difficult to steal it.

Elise entered the back porch of her aunt's home and found the clean linen cloths which she had left there for bathing. She lifted the cover off the cistern which, she had understood her uncle to say, was fed by an underground spring. The water was always clean and safe to drink. She found some scented soap nearby and began to bathe, rinsing off outside with jugs of water from the cistern. She remembered being told by her aunt that the fine soap was imported from Marseilles before the capture of New Orleans. She was even able to wash her hair after many weeks of being cooped up in the cave without water enough for a good bath and washing her hair.

Though the water was cold, she felt clean for the first time in many days, and she silently thanked the Lord for the cistern and the clean water. She had heard of people in town drinking water from mudholes and ditches. Some even sopped up the water with their blankets and squeezed the water into their mouths. She was also thankful that many soldiers and citizens, alike, could use her aunt's and uncle's cistern, though it was farther away than many were able to walk.

She wrapped a linen towel around herself and proceeded up the staircase inside to her room, where she hoped to change into some clean clothing. At the top of the stairs, she heard someone open the front door. Panicked, she crept to her room, hoping whoever it was would leave. However, when she heard steps on the stairway, she stifled a scream. It might be a no-good Yank, trying to steal everything in sight. She looked about for a place to hide, when she heard a voice at her door.

"Elise? Are you here? I didn't find you in the cave, so I was hoping to find you here." It was Stone. Before she could answer, he knocked on the door before opening it and walked into the room. He was not in uniform and she wondered why. She didn't know what to do. She clutched the large towel around herself as he walked over to her.

"I...I bathed a little," Elise said, feeling vulnerable and not knowing what to say or do.

"I see you did, Darling. I...I didn't know for sure that this was your room here. I'll leave, if you want me to." His eyes were looking at her as she drew the cloth even more tightly around herself. All she could think about was that she wanted to rest in his arms. She wanted to feel the safety of his arms and his mouth on hers again. She could only stand there as he walked over and put his arms around her. She held on to the towel, aware that only its thinness was between her body and his. He turned her face up to him and kissed her. Then, with his strong body trembling and his voice shaking and husky, he told her to get dressed. He would meet her downstairs, after she dressed.

Shutting the door behind him, Stone left the room. Elise dressed hurriedly, thankful to put on clean undergarments and a clean homespun dress. She found a hand towel and tried to dry her hair, then combed it, trying to straighten out the tangles. She took several dresses and underclothes from the armoire to carry back to the cave with her. Then, she hurried down the stairs to see Stone. Something in her mind told her that not many men would have left her untouched in such a compromising situation as she was in, without any clothes on. When she walked into the parlor, Stone was looking at the grand piano in the adjacent music room.

"Do you play, Elise?" he asked, glancing from her to the piano.

"Yes, I've had music lessons. I love to play."

"Let me hear you," he said.

Elise opened the hymnal on the beautiful Steinway piano, carved from French rosewood. It was a late addition to her aunt's home, and she was thankful that it was spared from the recent fire that consumed a wall of the music room. She began playing one of the hymns and to her surprise, Stone began to hum along as she played. She began singing along, also, and he soon joined in the singing. Tears came to her eyes because everything seemed so normal, not a peaceful moment in the midst of a death struggle. The tears rolled down her cheeks, and she felt herself being lifted from the piano bench into Stone's arms. He kissed her face and her lips and she felt his hands moving over her body before releasing her and finding a handkerchief to dry her tears.

"It seems I'm always providing a handkerchief for you," he said gently, as he wiped away her tears. "By the way, I walked here today. I don't want to subject Blackberry to the shelling. This war will soon be over soon, Elise, my dear," he continued, "and then I hope you will marry me."

Elise didn't know what to say. She could not imagine life now without missiles flying day and night and not having enough to eat and never having enough water in the cave. She didn't even know whether she would survive the war. She went into his arms and laid her head on his chest. Neither of them spoke, as he stroked her hair and her face.

"Will you marry me?" he finally said, holding her away from him and looking into her eyes.

"Yes," she said, as tears again came to her eyes.

"Well, we'll have something to look forward to, won't we?" he said, adding, "Now, I need to tell you something. I won't be able to come much in the days and weeks ahead. Please remember that I love you and we are planning to be married as soon as the war is over. I'm needed as an engineer now more than ever." After being sure that his words registered, by the expression on Elise's face, he said, "There may be some cabbages in your aunt's vegetable garden. Let's see if we can find some for you and your family and maybe for some of the other folks in your aunt's cave." Stone grabbed a large seed sack as they walked out the back door.

"Yes, Jack has brought us cabbage from the garden, but there should be some left, if the soldiers haven't taken all of them,"

Elise said. As they walked to the garden, she spied some unripe, half brown peaches which she picked, with Stone's help, and dropped into the large pockets of her dress.

"I think one sack of cabbages will be all we can manage this time, along with the water, but we'll see how many we can put in it," Stone said.

They finally reached the garden which was overgrown with weeds and the spent shells of war. However, several cabbages could be seen, which had survived being picked over by unknown persons. Before Elise could reach for one, Stone had filled the burlap seed sack with the only ones which could be found. He quickly tied the ends of the bag and reached for her hand. It was then that Elise thought to check on her aunt's and uncle's carriage.

"Stone, I need to check on the carriage in the coach house. The Percherons are gone, and I'm wondering whether someone took the carriage, also."

"Well, it would be difficult to do, but I guess it would be possible," Stone said, as they walked to the coach house. Stone opened the door which was unlocked, and they were shocked at what they saw. The carriage was completely destroyed, its lamps in a thousand bits of glass. Elise sobbed at the ruin of the once proud conveyance. Stone pulled her away from the scene of destruction and closed the door behind them. Elise wondered whether her uncle knew. She felt that it would be best not to tell her aunt about it. It would just be something else to add to her sadness and her sense of loss. Stone put his arm around Elise and walked with her to the back porch.

"Now, let's find some buckets for the water you came for," he said, gently. "Your aunt told me you had probably come up here for water."

"She was asleep when I left," Elise said, drying her eyes with the handkerchief which Stone pulled from his pocket, "and, yes, we always need more water!" she added, giving Stone back his handkerchief. "Also, I need to bring Aunt Celia some clothes. I'll only be a minute," she said, as she hurried to her aunt's room on the main floor. When she returned, Stone had found a large cloth bag to put the clothes in, and she helped to stuff them into the bag. These, he then tied around his neck and let the large bundle rest against his back for the downhill trip back to the cave.

Finding buckets on the porch, they both began filling them with the jugs Elise had brought from the cave. Stone carried two of the large buckets in each hand and Elise could only marvel that he was able to negotiate the steep embankment while carrying them, along with the sack of cabbages. She carried two of the filled jugs and it was all she could do to slip and slide back down the hill to the cave. How wonderful it would be to have more water in the cave!

As Stone carried the water into the cave, Elise and her Aunt Celia thanked him for helping them. He told her aunt that he was needed now more than ever by his regiment and wouldn't be able to come as much to see about them. He told them to stay in the cave as much as possible and to go outside the cave only during the times of the least shelling, from early morning, noon, and evening, when the Yanks were probably taking a break and letting their guns rest.

"I have something for you," he said, putting his hands in his pockets. He drew out some hardtack and coffee. Elise and her aunt both exclaimed over the coffee. When had they enjoyed a cup of coffee, instead of the improvised sweet potato and sassafras "coffee" which they had drunk since the siege began?

"You know," Celia Holmes said, "we've experimented with parched potatoes, burned meal, parched pindars, and roasted acorns, and some have found that okra coffee is the best, if we don't have the real thing, but there's nothing like a cup of true coffee.

People are saving the okra seeds for coffee. I haven't tried any of the okra coffee yet, and I don't plan to, but I'm looking forward to a cup of the real thing. Thank you, Stone!"

"You're welcome, Mrs. Holmes. If I can, I'll come back to check on you," Stone said, "but I understand that Grant has surrounded Vicksburg now, and the shelling will come from the East and the West. Also, I understand that Pemberton and Grant have agreed on a truce, so the bluecoats can bury their dead. It's supposed to last several hours today," Stone said, adding, "The effluvia from the putrefying bodies is unbearable to both sides." He urged both of them to be careful and with that, he was gone. Elise felt as if her life were gone, also, at his leaving.

Elise told her Aunt Celia that she was going to the Duff-Green hospital to see her mother and then to the market place to find them some food. She was not surprised that her aunt did not offer to go with her. Her Aunt Celia was not the strong, vigorous person she remembered from her childhood, especially now that her Uncle Alan could not visit them as often as he once did. So many of their soldiers were ill now, which made him especially needed in the trenches.

Tying a bonnet under her chin, Elise put her mother's clothing into the basket which she carried for any food she might find at the market place. She then hurried from the cave, fearful that at any moment the shelling would commence again. Other ladies of the town were scurrying around, also, their bonneted heads held low, as if to ward off enemy missiles.

Elise was shocked at the appearance of most of the homes. Whole panes in the windows were rare. Many of the houses were minus panes or had ones which had cracks and holes in them. One man was gathering up all the iron fragments and unburst shells in his neighborhood and was piling them into a sort of a monument in his front yard. Elise guessed that it would probably weigh a ton, at least.

Rats moved slowly about the town, looking for something to eat. Elise noticed how thin they were, though people were setting traps for them now in their own quest for something…anything…to eat. She also observed that very few dogs and cats were roaming the streets now. They had probably met the same fate as the rats, she thought with a heavy heart.

She walked hurriedly to the Duff-Green House. A yellow flag billowed in the slight breeze above the house. Operations were performed on the bottom level which originally housed the black servants of the family, along with the indoor kitchen, she had been told. It was likely the only house in town with an indoor kitchen, she thought. The Confederate wounded were housed on the middle floor, regarded as the first floor of the stately family dwelling. She remembered her Aunt Celia telling her that the housing of the Northern prisoners on the top floor made it less likely that the house would be hit by enemy missiles, the premise being that the bluecoats would not want to harm their compatriots, so they avoided shelling the house which was now a hospital.

Before she reached the door, the foul odor of blood and human waste, and the screams of pain, assailed her senses. Upon walking through the door, she stepped on the dirt first floor. An amputation was in progress. She could smell the laudanum and camphor and also the whiskey that the surgeon gave to his patients, attempting to allay the terrible pain of amputation.

Everyone in the room was busy and scarcely noticed Elise as she hurried to the stairs, afraid that she was going to faint. The scent of laudanum made her nauseated, and she held the bannister tightly as she climbed the steps to the second floor. At the open door to the room which held only women patients, she saw her mother sitting in a chair near her narrow cot. Her hands were busy with a large piece of homespun material which she was sewing, making each stitch a double one with a large needle.

Elise's first thought was that her mother had on the same bloodstained dress she was wearing when the ambulance transported her to the hospital several weeks before. Her second thought was wondering who had brought her mother the knitting needles and yarn which lay on a small table by her bed and, also, the homespun material which was occupying her mother's attention. As Abby Holmes looked up and saw her, Elise hurried over and hugged her.

"Mama, what are you doing?" she asked, looking at the homespun material in her mother's busy hands. Both looked at each other with tears in their eyes.

"Oh, Elise, it's so wonderful to see you, though I worry about your walking outside with all the shelling going on. What in the world is going to happen to all of us?" Abby Holmes said, before addressing the question Elise had asked. "I'm trying to make Jack a uniform. I never thought I'd be making a uniform, especially for Jack, at his age, but he wants one, now that his other one is too dirty and ragged to wear. He brought me a shirt of his and some pants for a pattern," she said, nodding to the shirt and pants at the foot of her cot.

When Abby motioned for her to sit on the nearby cot, Elise complied, smiling and shaking her head in amazement that her mother finally accepted the fact that her young son was in the trenches and considered himself a part of the fighting force of the Confederacy, relishing his duties as courier to the commanding general.

"I think I'm safe here, Elise. You probably know that the Yankee prisoners are up the stairs on the top floor. Our soldiers are guarding them. Once they're well enough, they're carried to the prison in town. I worry about you and Jack and Celia and Alan, but I'm probably safer here than anywhere else. The doctor said I should stay here the duration of the fighting here at Vicksburg, so my hip will heal. He thinks General Johnston is only about forty or fifty miles from here. He says Johnston is in Yazoo City now. He has thousands of soldiers with him. I wish he would hurry and end the siege on this town. Lord, have mercy…what is he waiting on?"

"I, too, wish he would come on, Mama. Yes, I saw the guards on the landing upstairs. You're right, Mama. You're probably safer here than anywhere else, since the Yanks won't shell this hospital where their soldiers are. We've been hearing that Johnston is on his way since we first came to Vicksburg. Why doesn't he come on?" Elise sat down near the foot of her mother's bed and began pulling her mother's clothes from the bag, as Abby set aside the unfinished uniform.

"Mama, I brought you some clothes. Let me help you put on another dress and petticoat."

"Well, since I'm in bed most of the time now, maybe a chemise and dress will be better."

"All right. I brought both for you, Mama," Elise said, as she helped her mother take off her soiled clothing and put on clean ones. She left the dirty clothes on the floor near her mother's bed, not knowing what else to do with them. They never had enough water to wash clothes in the cave and not enough time in the house with the shells flying around them.

"How are you all getting along in the cave, Elise?"

"We're doing all right, Mama. I'm thankful to have a place to go, away from the shells. Of course, now that Grant's army is on the eastern side of Vicksburg, it's even more dangerous because the shells can come right into our caves." As quickly as Elise made the comment, she regretted it, for her mother began sobbing and clutching Elise's arm, as if she were trying to find shelter from the enemy. Elise quickly changed the subject, and she saw her mother dry her tears.

"Mama, where did you get the knitting needles and the pretty skeins of yarn," she asked, "and also the homespun?" Her mother's eyes brightened as she replied, "Isabel brought them to me. They're some that she had."

"Oh, how sweet and thoughtful," Elise said.

"Yes, she's always been that way," Abby said.

"Are you getting enough to eat?" Elise asked.

"We have cornbread and bacon most days, sometimes three times a day. Sometimes, we have peameal and hardtack. What are you and Celia eating?"

"We, too, are eating hardtack and cornbread and bacon when we can get it," Elise said.

"You have lost weight, Elise. I declare, it seems everyone in Vicksburg has lost weight. Maybe we all can hold out until Johnston comes. We keep hearing he's coming, but he just never gets here." Elise wanted to say that she didn't believe that Johnston would ever come, but she refrained, not wanting to take any hope away from her mother.

"Well, Mama," she said, instead, "I've got to hurry before the heavy shelling starts again. I'm on my way to the market. I've heard there's mule meat for sale now. I've never eaten it, but they say it's not bad when you can't get any other kind of meat. Actually, it's a wonder any mules are left, as 1600 were recently driven over to the Yankees' side, because they were starving."

Noticing the surprised expression on her mother's face, Elise was going to explain about the mules when Jack bounded into the room, first giving his mother a kiss, then giving his sister a quick hug. Elise noticed that he had discarded the dirty Confederate uniform and now wore his own clothes which were showing wear and tear and also dirt. He appeared to be excited and in a hurry. However, when he saw the progress which his mother had made in sewing his uniform, he had to pick up the shirt and hold it against his chest.

"It'll be ready in about three more days, Jack, dear," Abby Holmes said, and Jack told his mother how very much he appreciated her making it for him, before telling them the reason for his hurried visit.

"Pemberton and Grant have agreed on a three-hour truce!" he exclaimed. "The dead bluecoats are causing such a stench in the town that Pemberton sent a flag of truce, so Grant's men can remove their dead. There shouldn't be any shelling this afternoon, Sis, so you should be safe as you walk about in town. Also, I have seen things I never expected to see in this war," he said, as Elise and Abby looked questioningly at him. "I've been over to the truce lines, where all of the white flags are, and I've seen things that I've never heard of," he continued.

"What? What are you talking about?" Elise asked.

"I've seen the Yanks burying their dead, but you won't believe what else is going on. Let me tell you that I have seen things I never expected to see in a war!" As Elise and Abby stared at him, he resumed his narrative.

"Yanks and Rebs were playing some sports together. I saw it with my own eyes. Then, I saw a card game in progress…two Yanks and two Rebs. Some of the Yanks gave us some food from their own rations, and they gave some to me." Jack quit talking and pulled some food from his haversack. "Here's some fat meat, crackers, and coffee," he said, giving some of it to his mother and Elise. Elise and Abby were shocked as they looked at the food Jack had given them.

"This is hard to believe, Jack." Elise said as she put her share of the food into her basket. Abby put hers on the table by her bed.

"I'll have some good coffee in the morning. No, I may not wait till morning. I may ask the orderly here to make me some coffee now, if he can get a fire going," Abby said, with an expression of delight, which her children hadn't seen on her face since the war began. Jack kissed his mother on the cheek again and as Elise and her mother said their goodbyes to him, he bolted from the door of the room and down the stairs. Now, it was Elise's time to go.

"I love you, Mama," Elise said, reaching over and kissing her mother. "If the shelling stops long enough again, I'll be back."

"I love you, too. I want you to stay in that cave and be safe, Elise. Oh, I meant to tell you, Elise, Stone Jackson has come several times to see me. He always brings me news of you and Celia. He rarely mentions Alan and Jack now, as he used to, but they're probably in a different regiment from him. He brought me some cooked salt water mackerel several weeks ago from some, he said, he had brought to you and Celia, and he has brought me something to eat other times, even if it's only hardtack. He seems quite fond of you, Elise."

Elise wanted to spill out the plans that she and Stone had made about marriage, but something caused her to refrain. Things were so unsettled, so unsure. They might not even be living when the war was over. Somehow, the time wasn't right to tell her mother all that she and Stone were planning. Instead, she kissed her mother again and told her goodbye, then left the room. She could hear her mother's voice as she headed back down the stairs.

"You stay safe, Elise!" Elise decided to take her mother's advice. She'd go another day to the market. She had enough food to last a few days. As she hurried toward the cave, she thought about the wailing that could be heard throughout the city. It sounded like women's voices which never let up, a constant cry of grief and pain. It grieved her heart to hear it.

Chapter Six

Cave life was bearable only because the people who were forced to live in the dugouts, or ratholes as they were called, made it so. Elise marveled at her aunt's ability to gather not only the occupants of the other rooms of her own cave but also those in nearby caves to meet together for singing, conversation, music, and Bible readings. Though Elise didn't know anyone, except Drusie and her mother, Isabel, she realized that her Aunt Celia knew not only everyone in the caves but everyone's black servants, also.

Elise especially enjoyed seeing the children who became well trained in their own survivals during the ongoing siege. In the daytime, during hours when the shelling was light, the young ones looked for blackberries and papaws and climbed trees, but when the iron hail flew in rapid succession, they scampered back to the caves like rabbits to their burrows. Sometimes, the older children gathered bunches of wildflowers or bright leaves which their mothers put in tin cups in the niches of the walls of their caves.

Elise had found some children's books at her aunt's home, ones which were read to her when she was a child, and she brought these back to the cave to read to the children. She would hold one child while others gathered around to hear stories from the books which she read out loud. As the missiles shrieked above them, this always brought calm to herself, as well as the children. She wondered whether she would live to have little ones of her own.

One evening when shrapnel, hot shot, grape, Parrott shells and Minie balls kept up a steady barrage of havoc and death, the occupants of the nearby caves gathered at the Holmes' cave, seeking companionship and comfort from one another. Some brought chairs through the twisting corridors of the caves, while others without seats simply sat on the floor of the dugout. Elise went around the room, lighting candles and lanterns. Drusie and Isabel Davis, along with their black servants, were among the group. Three dogs and several cats lay on the floor by their owners or walked about the cave. They shivered and crouched and some howled as the missiles flew overhead.

Several of the men who were too old to fight or had health issues which precluded their joining the Rebel army, had brought their musical instruments and proceeded to play together some of the songs of the times. One man with his prized violin began playing the song "Lorena" which caused a hush to fall over the cave room. The man's young daughter held the sheet music before him and turned the pages as he played. Celia Holmes whispered to Elise to find the lyrics to the song, which she had brought from her aunt's home only several days prior. She had found the sheet music, which also had the lyrics, in the bench of the grand piano, as her aunt had requested, and she had brought them back to their cave.

After Elise retrieved the music from the cave room which she shared with her aunt, several gathered around her, singing the words to the music of the violin. When missiles caused the cave to shake, they stopped singing only momentarily, until they realized the cave was holding steady. Others in the cave constantly waved their hand fans to ward off mosquitoes and flies and gnats. Those nearest the musicians and singers alternately fanned them and also themselves.

When the musicians put away their instruments, the older man, who along with his wife were living in a room of the Holmes' cave, was asked by Celia Holmes to read the Bible and to pray for all of them. Different ones in the group, who had brought Bibles, turned to the text he selected and followed along as he read. Someone held a candle near the reader's Bible, in order for him to see to read. After closing his Bible, he prayed for everyone and asked the Lord to keep everyone safe and to bring an end to the war. Elise noticed that he did not pray for the South's victory, and she wondered why.

After the meeting, different ones began telling their cave experiences. One woman told about seeing something moving at the bottom of one of the post supports of the roof of their cave. It proved to be a large snake, wrapped around the post. Another person told of a snake found between some mattresses where she had slept since the siege began. Others told about the rats that prowled the caves. Elise had seen the thin rats, also, creeping around from room to room in the caves, looking for food. Some of the cave occupants were trapping them now for food.

Someone spoke up and said that rats were hanging dressed in the marketplace in town. People were actually eating them, along with mule meat. Elise shuddered at the thought of eating rats or mule meat, but she knew that if she became hungry enough, she might have to succumb to eating almost anything. She had even heard of people boiling and eating shoe leather. What were they coming to? When would this cruel war be over? She looked down at herself and knew that she was becoming thinner and thinner, as was everyone in the room.

As the iron hail rained thunder of incendiary shells, now coming from both the East and the West, one of the men in the group pulled a newspaper from his pocket and offered to read an article about the shells that were flying above them. The cave shook from the fiery cannonade above it. Everyone listened eagerly as he read from the Citizen newspaper about the shells which flew over them:

"These shells contain a small tin tube, about the size of an ounce vial, which appears to be filled with some ignitable fluid, and is wrapt around on the outside with several layers of paper. Upon the bursting of the shell, the top of the tube is blown off and the fluid ignited. When it falls upon the ground it burns with a blue, flickering blaze some two minutes and seems to possess intense heat, consuming the green grass within its reach."

Just as the man finished reading from the newspaper, Jack suddenly appeared in the cave. Though Elise was happy to see him, she was absolutely flabbergasted to see the gray slouch hat with the incongruously large red feather he was wearing. She decided not to question him about the hat until another time, when they were alone, but she found it difficult not to stare at it. She had an idea where he had gotten it, and she couldn't help the smile that spread across her face when she looked at it.

Though Jack seemed to be excited and literally bursting with news about the progress of the war, he first gave Elise and his Aunt Celia perfunctory hugs and pecks on their cheeks. Everyone waited in suspense, wanting to hear what he had to say. Swallowing hard several times and obviously trying to catch his breath, he blurted out the news he came to tell.

"First of all, General Johnston is above Yazoo City with 22,000 men. That's some really good news. Also, General Pemberton has gotten word somehow that the ironclad Cincinnati is heading down the river past our batteries in the morning." As everyone in the crowded room looked at one another, Jack continued:

"Well, we have an 11-piece heavy artillery battery on the bluff above the Cincinnati. The Feds know it was there, but they think it's been removed and is no longer there. Actually, it is still there, but the guns have been lowered in their carriages, so they're not visible from the ironclad. They're still there!" Elise could tell that Jack was filled with pride in the Confederate's deception of the Yankees. This would be a battle that the Rebs would win. Before anyone could ask any questions, Jack continued with the news that he had especially wanted to tell them.

"If you want to see the bluecoats lose a battle, then go to any of the high bluffs in the morning. You'll see the Yanks outwitted, for sure. Oh," he continued, "Uncle Alan says the 'Whistling Dick' is the main part of the battery! He says its ball has a steel point and is two and a half feet long and weighs 250 pounds. Wait'll you hear the noise it makes when it's fired! Whoo- eee!"

Clapping erupted from everyone in the cave, as Jack turned to leave. However, Elise told him firmly that he needed to spend the night in the cave. She didn't want him to make a return trip to the trenches with bullets flying around the city. He said he had found his way to the cave by the light of the many fires burning in the city, caused by the constant shelling of the Union Army and naval fleet. Elise told him that made him a moving target, and he looked relieved not to have to make the return trip to the trenches until the next morning. Elise promised to let him have one of the mattresses on her cot for a bed.

When morning came, Elise found that Jack had already left for the trenches. She and several of the ladies in the nearby rooms of the cave decided to make the trip to Sky Parlor Hill to watch the doom of the warship Cincinnati from the safety of the steep cliff. Her aunt not wanting to make the lengthy walk, Elise left her with her crochet needle and several skeins of yarn which Elise had retrieved for her from her house above the cave. Elise promised to tell her all about the fate of the Yankee ironclad Cincinnati when she returned.

The rain of overhead shelling had all but ceased when Elise and Drusie and Isabel Davis left their caves and walked toward Sky Parlor Hill. Other women joined them along the way, fearlessly ignoring the positive orders of their military not to expose themselves to the thunderous missiles of the enemy. It wasn't long before they arrived at Sky Parlor Hill which was filled with people, mostly women, looking through their spy glasses at the ironclad warship Cincinnati up the river from them. Awaiting orders to begin its mission down the river, its squat shape and slanted sides resembled a large turtle whose stern and pilot house were protected with bales of hay.

Elise could not help but notice the beauty of the scene on both sides of the river below them, so at odds with the death and ruination that she saw and dealt with each day. Sycamore, willow, and cypress trees, draped with long moss hanging from their branches, were covered with buds. Birds of all kinds were chirping in the trees. She saw a flock of parrots flying over the tree tops to the Louisiana side of the river. In the distance beyond them, to the east of the town, they all could see several plantations where Rebels were burning their cotton to keep it from falling into enemy hands.

As the monster ship left its moorings and headed downriver, its crew met with a deadly surprise when the Confederates at Fort Hill raised the guns in their hidden carriages and opened fire. The first shell from the "Whistling Dick," the pride of the Confederacy, appeared to score a direct hit, exiting possibly through the bottom of the ship, while another shell apparently disabled the ship's steering mechanism. Not able to elevate the Cincinnati's own guns to return fire to the high battery on the hill, and realizing that his ship was doomed, the commander of the Cincinnati tried to head his ship, full-steam, back up the river.

Elise could see splinters sailing through the air as the Rebel guns continued to fire on the warship. Some of the splinters almost flew up to the bluffs where many were watching the battle. She knew that those on the ship, who were hit by these wood missiles, would suffer terrible wounds.

When the Cincinnati headed up the Mississippi, the ladies on the hills above the river cheered until their voices were hoarse, all the while waving their handkerchiefs as the warship began to sink in deep water. The U.S. flag was frantically removed several times by the Union soldiers on-board, first from the aft mast, then the main mast, and lastly the forward mast, its final resting place being on the stump of the forward mast.

As others on the bluff at Sky Parlor Hill hailed the sinking of the Cincinnati, Elise cheered alongside them and joined all of them in waving their handkerchiefs. Isabel Davis and Drusie picked up the huge Confederate flag which was positioned on the cliff and waved it in the face of the enemy.

Elise could see blue-coated men floundering in the water, some who obviously could not swim. She saw some men swimming toward shore, pulling their sinking comrades along beside them. She saw one man on a hay bale, floating down the river toward the Rebel entrenchments. Some on-board the sinking ship shot at him, perhaps thinking he was fleeing the Union Army. Though others on the high bluff continued in joyfully hailing the sinking of the Union ironclad, Elise felt only horror as she witnessed many of Union men flailing in deep water and ultimately drowning.

~ O ~

That evening, the sinking of the Cincinnati was the main news of the day, as the nearby cave occupants met once again in the Holmes' cave. One of the men who was on crutches because of an amputated leg, had heard from his brother in the trenches that the crew of the Cincinnati had lost five killed or mortally wounded, fourteen injured by Rebel fire, and fourteen dead by drowning. It was a major victory for the Rebs! Someone in the group asked the man whose name was Mr. Cravey what guns of the Rebels actually sank the Cincinnati.

"My brother said the battery on the hill had the Whistling Dick, also the Blakely rifle, called the Widow Blakely, and the Brooke rifle. Which one sank the gunboat? Only God knows. I'd bet on the Whistling Dick, but it was probably a combination of the three I named, plus others. Our boys have given us a victory that we all can be proud of! Oh…and…Dad-burn it! I heard that the gunboat had about $25,000 worth of our cotton on board!"

Someone asked, "Well, what happened to the fellow who floated down the river on the hay bale?"

"Oh, our boys got 'im for sure. He's a prisoner now. Ol' Grant was outsmarted today, somethin' he'll never forget!"

Isabel Davis brought some taffy which she had managed to make on the fire pit outside her cave. She told everyone in attendance that she used the last of their butter and sugar to make the candy, but she wanted to bring something special to celebrate the Rebels' winning the morning battle. Ruefully, she admitted that she usually added a little salt to the mixture but she had no salt to add.

At this admission, everyone in the cave bemoaned the fact that they hadn't had salt to add to their little bit of food for several weeks. Elise was surprised when one of the men in attendance, named Ben Smith, spoke up about the salt shortage.

"I read somewhere that you can rip out the floorboard of your smokehouses and soak the boards in water and then boil the water to extract the salt," he said.

"Well, Ben," Celia Holmes said, "I'd be glad for someone to extract the salt from our smokehouse. Also, there are troughs and barrels in the kitchen, which were used for meat brining. You might get some salt from those."

"All right, York and Luge and Mack," Ben Smith said, addressing his colored servants, "you heard Mrs. Holmes…that's something we can do tomorrow. I reckon we all need salt."

"Yes," Celia continued, "there's water in the cistern on the back porch, and you can find some large boilers in the kitchen to soak the planks. Also, you can boil the water in the kitchen. You can make a fire from the wood in the rail fence."

After this was settled, Celia suggested that Isabel mount the taffy on the wall, so the children, and any adults who wanted to, could pull it. Five children in the group, including the two young daughters of Mrs. Sybil Adams, held out their hands to be washed by their mothers, then waited for Isabel Davis to coat them with the little bit of butter, which she had saved for just such a special occasion.

Elise noticed how thin Mrs. Adams looked, though her stomach was distended. Her third child would soon be born, and it would be born in a cave. Her husband had died in the trenches several weeks before, leaving his wife to go through childbirth and the rearing of their children alone. She did not appear to have any close family nearby.

After the children had pulled the taffy, rendering it the right consistency, Celia Holmes found some scissors and cut pieces for everyone in the cave room. As they enjoyed the taffy, one of the ladies, named Mrs. Wilkins, produced several newspapers which had articles of interest. She told everyone that the papers had been brought across the Mississippi River in the dark of night by expert swimmers who dared to swim near the Union gunboats. All in the cave leaned forward to hear the latest news. Mrs. Wilkins opened one of the newspapers.

"This is from the *Cincinnati Gazette*," she said:

"A lady from Shelbyville, arrived today, says that a report of the surrender of Vicksburg was prevalent in the rebel camp. A later arrival confirms the existence of the rumor and the same person states that the rebel papers had published the particulars of the capitulation."

Folding that paper and passing it around to the ones in the cave, she opened another paper. "This is from the *Washington Evening Star*," she said:

"Rumors of disaster at Vicksburg and Port Hudson have been afloat today, but we are unable to obtain any information in the absence of which they may be set down as canards."

"This last one I have is from the *Jackson Mississippian*":

"Through mistake, a report which was nothing more than street talk, crept into our edition yesterday, stating that a large force of Confederate cavalry had entered Vicksburg." As everyone in the cave sat quietly, trying to digest this latest news, a Mr. Couper held up two newspapers and read from one of them."

"This is from the *Philadelphia Bulletin*," he said:

"A lady who came within our lines states that the rebels are in receipt of very depressing news from Vicksburg and that well- known rebels in Chattanooga and Shelbyville are selling off their goods and property to noncombatants at great sacrifices, in anticipation of our speedy occupation of those places…"

After reading this and passing it around, he held up a strip of wallpaper which held an article from the local *Citizen* newspaper. Out of newsprint, the editor now resorted to printing on the reverse side of wallpaper. As his wife held a candle for him to read, Mr. Couper read from the small strip of wallpaper which measured about one and a half feet by six inches:

"The enemy's mortar batteries on the opposite side of the river have been studiously pouring their bursting shells into a certain part of the city the past 25 days. So far, in proportion to the immense mass of destructive missiles hurled in our midst, very little damage has been done, save in our hospitals. Towards these buildings, now the majority in the city, the enemy directs his special attention; and wherever a yellow flag – the emblem of the sick and wounded and suffering – is visible, there the humane Yankee directs his one-sided, dastardly warfare. We cannot point to an instance of savage-like, barbarian, cowardly assault as these mortar batteries exhibit. Knowing as the enemy must that our city is inhabited solely by helpless women and children, sick, wounded and dying, still he exhibits an ultra-inhuman persistence and butcher-thugism…how long, how long, oh Lord! Shall we witness these acts of the barbarian?"

As he finished reading, Elise said a silent prayer, thanking the Lord that her mother was in a hospital that was rarely attacked by the enemy, since the enemy prisoners were held on its top floor. When Mr. Couper finished reading from the strip of wallpaper and had rolled it into a small wad which he stuffed into his shirt pocket, he volunteered that he had heard on the streets of Vicksburg that Grant had recently acquired several large siege guns. Each gun required ten yoke of oxen to haul it to its place. It was said that the balls from these monsters could be seen when they were shot toward the town.

Elise felt a shiver run through her body at this revelation, and when she looked around the candlelit cave, she saw fear and despair on the faces of everyone. Would the siege ever end? She had forgotten what they were fighting over. Oh, yes, it was slavery. But hadn't Ben Smith's black servants been true to him? Hadn't they been helpful to all of them? Some said they were fighting over states' rights. She wondered whether she would live to see the end of the conflict.

What Elise had feared most, after the shelling of the enemy, came to pass the next morning. She was awakened by a loud clap of thunder and the crack of lightning, as a storm drenched the war-ravaged city. With enough lightning to see by, she lit a candle and also a lantern in the cave room. Her Aunt Celia also awoke and looked at Elise, as if to ask what they should do.

Water was now inching its way under the sheet curtain in their dugout room, and Elise wondered what they should do, also. She and her aunt had both slept in the clothing they had worn the evening before, so they didn't have to change from night clothes which they never wore anymore. They both hurriedly put on their stockings and shoes.

"Aunt Celia, maybe we should go into the large room and sit in the chairs there," Elise said, as she picked up the lit candle and glowing lantern. Without uttering a sound, her aunt followed Elise into the main room of the cave.

Elise was surprised but grateful to see the three Negro servants of Ben Smith sloshing around in the water which now covered the cave floor. Two of the servants, York and Luge, found blocks of wood for Elise and her aunt to rest their feet on, out of the water. The servant named Mack addressed her aunt about carving a fire pit in the wall of the cave. He explained that they could temporarily use it for cooking and also the heat from the fire should dry the water in the cave, once the rain stopped. Celia agreed to this and nodded toward the shovel in the corner of the room, which he could use to hollow out a fire pit.

Finding some dry kindling in another room of the cave and some dry wood from the rail fence, which luckily someone had thought to bring to the cave before the rain set in, the servants started the fire and managed to cook bacon and hoecakes for the occupants of the Holmes' cave. Though the heat was oppressive, the rain soon ceased and the exposed areas of the cave walls and floor began to dry out. Elise looked at the walls and ceiling of the cave and noticed hairline cracks that she hadn't seen before. She could only pray that the cave wouldn't collapse on all of them.

As Elise was making plans for the day, now that the rain had ceased, Alan Holmes made a rare visit to the cave. Celia Holmes wept as her husband hugged and kissed her and also kissed

Elise on the cheek.

"I came to check on you. It's good to see you both are doing well."

"Yes, Alan," Celia Holmes said, "Ben's servants dug a fire pit on the wall, as you can see," she said, pointing to the hollowed-out cooking pit on the wall. "They made all of us some breakfast, too. They are good colored folks."

"Well, I see they did it just right," Alan Holmes said, adding, "I'm glad they're looking after you." After the conversation about the raised fireplace, Elise was puzzled to see tears in her uncle's eyes.

"I came to check on you, also to get some clothes for Jack. He said he didn't want to wear any dry clothes, when others were standing in water, some with little strips of carpet pulled around them and others with nothing but their thin, saturated clothes which cling to them. There they lie, or stand, all day in the water, with only a meal from yesterday to give them any strength. I'm going to the house now to get him some clothes. Do you want me to bring anything back for you?" He quickly pulled a handkerchief from his pocket and wiped his eyes before shoving it again into his pocket.

"No, we're all right, Uncle Alan," Elise said. "However, I do want to ask you something. Where in the world did Jack get his hat with the big red feather?"

Alan Holmes grinned…the first time Elise had seen such an expression on her uncle's face since the siege began. "Stone Jackson found it somewhere and gave it to Jack," he said. Elise had thought this all along, that Stone had given the hat to her brother. It made Jack happy and it made her happy for her brother to be happy. Also, she loved Stone for making three of her family smile when they looked at the hat. It was something to take their minds off of the siege and the possibility of starvation which they faced each day.

"Jack said for me to bring as many of his clothes back as I could, so some of the other men would have something dry to wear." Elise realized at that moment how close Jack and their uncle had become.

After saying his goodbyes, with tears from each of them, Alan Holmes left the cave, followed by his wife and Elise. They watched him as he began the arduous climb up the hill to his house. Before entering his back porch, he turned and gave them a final wave. Elise realized with certainty that the war had brought her uncle and her brother so close that Alan Holmes now regarded Jack as the son he never had.

The rest of the day passed uneventfully, though the shelling continued without any letup. Just before sundown, Jack paid them a visit. Elise noticed that he had on dry clothes, and she silently thanked her uncle for insisting that he wear them. He also wore the gray hat with the large red feather. Elise seized the moment to ask him about the feather.

"Jack, I like your hat, especially the red feather. Uncle Alan said that Stone gave it to you."

"He did," Jack said with a grin on his face. "Stone said, 'You've needed a hat, little brother, and some decoration for it, too.'" He called me "little brother," Jack said, still grinning. Elise smiled at him and told him that the red feather did indeed decorate the plain hat.

Then, she saw that Jack was holding some trinkets which he said he had carved from their parapet wood and from Minie balls, which were a little chair and a small plow. These he gave to Elise, asking her to give them to the Adams children, Carrie and Adeline, who lived with their mother down the back hallway from the Holmes' cave. Jack also had a live plaything for the children, a small bird which he found fluttering around near his battery. He set the little bird down on the floor of the cave, and it commenced hopping around the dugout.

"Well, I gotta go, Sis," Jack said. "Please give the carvings and the bird to the little girls."

"I will, Jack. I didn't know you could carve like this," Elise said with a look of admiration at the small trinkets he had created.

"Something to pass the time while the bullets fly," Jack said, ruefully, adding as he gave her a quick peck on her cheek, "You and Aunt Sissy, be careful…take care of yourselves."

"We will, Jack. Aunt Celia is taking a nap. She sleeps a lot now," Elise said, as Jack threw up his hand and left the cave.

Elise stared at the little bird as it hopped around on the floor of the cave. She had never held a bird, but she picked it up, marveling at its lightness. Putting the carvings in her pocket, she grabbed a lantern and carried it and the tiny bird with her as she walked through the labyrinth of shadowy halls in the cave to where the Adams family was staying.

She always dreaded having to walk the narrow and low-ceilinged halls of the caves. Feelings of suffocation made her feel faint, and she found it difficult to breathe. Too, sometimes snakes and spiders took up residency in the dark, confined corridors.

The odor of unemptied chamber pots assailed her senses. She thought about the fact that the servants who remained in the caves with their owners were the ones who emptied and cleaned the waste pots. Now that most of the servants were gone, no one seemed to want to clean their own pots, or they feared the bullets when they stepped outside their caves, thereby leaving them filled with the smell of human waste.

As she crept along the shadowy clay hallway, several rats brushed past her, their beady eyes darting here and there, looking for a crumb to eat and nearly causing her to drop all that she carried. Their high-pitched squeaks added to the horror of the cave, and she wished then that she could wash herself from the contact with the rodents. Those who ate them tried to mitigate the horror of ingesting them by calling the dish "squirrel stew." As she crept along with her head lowered, she heard the sounds of living from other nearby caves...the heated arguments and the intimate words and sounds that lacked privacy and made her blush. She could hear the Adams children fussing and complaining, as she stood before the makeshift curtain which served as a door to the back part of their cave, and called out to them.

Mrs. Adams pulled aside the curtain and welcomed Elise on her first visit to their dugout. Glad to be able finally to stand up straight in the cave room, Elise was shocked by her neighbor's appearance. She remembered how her mother had looked only a day or so before her brother Jeremy was born, and Mrs. Adams had the same appearance. Her eyes were puffy and her midriff huge. Her eyes fastened on the bird which Elise held.

"My brother Jack brought some trinkets he had carved and this tiny bird for your girls," Elise said, first handing the trinkets to the girls whose eyes opened wide as they accepted them.

"Thank you, Miss Elise," they chimed in almost simultaneously, eyeing the little chair and plow which Jack had created. However, they quickly placed the trinkets on the table in the room and gazed at the little bird which Elise placed on the floor, where it hopped and fluttered its wings. Carrie, the older child, picked it up and held it to her heart as her mother admonished her to be careful with it.

"I am, Mama. I'm being careful," she said. Now, Adeline reached up her arms, following her sister around the cave room.

"It's my turn," she cried, holding out her hands, but Carrie wouldn't part with the tiny bird.

"Take turns now," Mrs. Adams said. "Remember, we take turns, Carrie; it's Adeline's turn now," their mother said. Reluctantly, Carrie gave the little bird to her younger sister who sat on a cot and held it, as it chirped. Elise couldn't help but notice how thin the mother and two daughters looked. The mother's delivery of her third child was imminent, and Elise wondered where a midwife might be found to help her when the time came.

"If I don't see Jack, please tell him 'thank you' for thinking of my girls and carving the little chair and plow for them…also, the little bird. As you can see, they are captivated with it. They'll have many happy hours playing with these," she said with a smile.

"I'll tell him, Mrs. Adams," Elise said. As she was about to leave, Carrie spoke up.

"I think we have a name for our bird," she said, smiling with her teeth showing.

"What are you going to name the little fellow?" her mother asked with a smile.

"Twiggy," said Carrie. "His name is Twiggy because his legs look like twigs," she giggled.

"That's a good name," Elise said with a smile as she left the cave room. She could hear the children laughing and playing as she walked back to the Holmes' cave. It surprised and pleased her that Jack would do something for the two children, and she mulled over the fact that he had matured so much in only a few weeks' time.

Returning to the main room of the Holmes' cave, Elise saw several packets which someone had left on the table by the dugout entrance. She could tell from the aroma in the damp cave air that it was food! When she opened a packet and found fried salt mackerel, she knew that Stone Jackson had sent it to them. There was enough cooked fish and cornbread and bacon for everyone in the Holmes' cave. She pulled aside the curtain to the room in the cave, which she shared with her aunt but, as usual, her aunt was asleep. Elise knew it wasn't normal for her aunt to sleep so much, but she felt that maybe she could tune out the shattering noises of war which threatened the sanity and the well-being of all who occupied the caves in the town.

She couldn't help but wonder where Stone had gotten the food. No one else seemed to have access to so much food. He was actually keeping her and her family alive! The usual tears came to her eyes when she looked down at the shapeless frock that mostly hid her bones. She longed to go to him and, if they both survived the war, to spend the rest of her life with him.

She was so hungry, and the smell of food so tantalizing, that it took all of her willpower to refrain from eating it at once, to gulp it down. However, she apportioned the food for everyone in the Holmes' cave. The three black servants of the Ben Smith family had walked over to the Union side in the past week, so they wouldn't receive a portion of the food. They had made their escape under the guise of rendering salt from her aunt's smokehouse floor. The other occupants of the Holmes' cave were either in town trying to find food amid the constant shelling or visiting others in other parts of the linking caves. She left their portions in their rooms.

Elise sat alone in the main room of the cave and ate the food that was left. Tears of appreciation flooded her eyes as she ate, especially enjoying the salty taste of the mackerel. She hadn't eaten anything salty in many days. Again, she wondered how Stone could have access to such food. She could only hope that her family and all of their soldiers and the citizenry of the town had the food that she was eating. She knew that the siege of Vicksburg was threatening the lives of its people with starvation. When would it all be over…and who would be left alive? She sighed as she ate the crumbs and thanked God and Stone Jackson for the first good meal she had eaten in weeks.

Chapter Seven

The scream shattered the darkness of the night, and Elise awoke in fear. Had someone's cave fallen in? Had a shell killed someone? As she hurriedly tied her shoelaces, she glanced at her aunt who still slept.

Another scream pierced the night and Elise traced it to the Adams' cave. As she had feared, the time had come for the third child of the Adams family to make its entrance into the world, a world now torn by war and strife and hunger. When she stepped into the main room of their cave, she was surprised that others weren't roused by the noise, but they slept on like her Aunt Celia. Having left a candle burning for her aunt, if she should awaken, Elise took a lantern with her. It would give light to navigate the dark corridors to the Adams' cave.

The anguished screams came more regularly now, coupled with the sounds of Carrie and Adeline, as they cried out each time their mother screamed. When Elise finally reached the curtain of the Adams' cave, she called to the children. Both children pulled the curtain aside for her to enter. Their eyes were wide with fear, and tears rolled down their cheeks.

A small candle provided the only light in the room. Mrs. Adams lay on her cot, her hands gripping its sides and her face beaded with sweat. She looked at Elise but before she could speak, her face became contorted with pain, and another animal cry issued from her throat. She cast a helpless look at Elise who stood by her cot, not knowing what to do or how to help.

"My children, Miss Holmes...please see about my

children," she panted. The two girls clung to Elise who tried to think what she should do. Laying the lantern aside, she saw water in a basin nearby and she wet a cloth with it. With the girls still clinging to her, she wrung out the water and placed the damp cloth on their mother's forehead, then wiped her face with it.

"Do you know where I can find a midwife?" Elise asked.

"No, but Mrs. Davis might help me," Mrs. Adams said, slurring her words in her pain. "My girls…please take my girls with you." Her words were followed with a bout of quick, heavy breathing as her hands clutched the sides of her cot.

"I'm going to get Mrs. Davis," Elise said as she grabbed the lantern and ushered Carrie and Adeline through the back door of the cave. When she looked back at Mrs. Adams, she was trying to say "Thank you" when another paroxysm of pain brought about another scream.

The two little girls held onto Elise as she guided them back to her aunt's cave. She was pleased to see her Aunt Celia sitting in the main room of the cave. She had a questioning look on her face as she stared at Elise and the Adams girls.

"Is it Mrs. Adams' time?" she asked.

"Yes, Aunt Celia," Elise answered, adding, "Please keep Carrie and Adeline with you. I'm going to the Davis' cave to get Mrs. Isabel. Mrs. Adams said that Mrs. Isabel might help her."

"Well, I might be able to help, also, but she knows Isabel better. Their homes are right by each other. Well, come here, Carrie and Adeline," Celia Holmes said as she rose from her chair and moved toward the settee in the room. Both girls ran to the settee and sat on either side of Elise's aunt who put her arms around them. Their tears had ceased but their young faces were pinched with anxiety and fear for their mother.

As Elise started toward the door of the cave, the shelling seemed to become even more intense, and she feared making the walk to the Davis' dugout. Since it was several cave openings down from the Holmes' cave, she knew she would be a target because of the light and fires burning all over the city from the intense shelling.

"Be careful, Elise, precious," her aunt said, and tears came to Elise's eyes as she realized that her aunt feared for her safety, also. She looked back and saw tears in her beloved aunt's eyes as she cradled the two girls beside her.

"You be careful," she reiterated, "I'll look after Carrie and Adeline."

"I'll be back soon," Elise said, as she walked out of the cave into the night. She left the lantern with her aunt, as the moon and the fires burning all over the town provided enough light for her to walk to the Davis' cave. The missiles deafened her with their nearness and their roar.

Upon entering the dark Davis' cave, she saw a soft glow behind the coverlet which served as a curtain for the room which Mrs. Davis and Drusie shared. Elise could hear the muffled sounds of sleep emanating from the room, and she regretted having to disturb their few hours of peace from the stress and tumult of war. In spite of her qualms, however, Mrs. Adams urgently needed help. "Mrs. Isabel...Drusie?" she called out. Again, she called out, as she heard one or both of them stirring and trying to wake up.

"Yes, what is it," Isabel Davis answered. The curtain suddenly moved, with Drusie holding it to one side.

"Elise! What's the matter?" she asked, her eyes round with surprise.

"It's Mrs. Adams. She needs your mother, Drusie. It's her time, and she's in a lot of pain."

"I have some chloroform," Isabel Davis said, as she quickly roused from her cot and pulled on her stockings and shoes. She then held the curtain while Drusie laced up her shoes. Both of them joined Elise, with Isabel Davis carrying a bottle of chloroform.

The three of them hurried back to the Holmes' cave as enemy missiles lit up the night sky above them. When they entered the Holmes' cave, Elise saw that her Aunt Celia and the girls were gone. She pulled back the curtain to the room she shared with her aunt, and she saw all three of them asleep on her aunt's cot.

Elise picked up her lantern and motioned for Isabel Davis and Drusie to follow her. As they entered the narrow passageway that connected the rooms, Elise could hear once again the moans and screams of Mrs. Adams. Elise called out before entering the room with Drusie and her mother. She placed her lantern beside the candle, and the added light made the room less dismal and gloomy.

Sybil Adams silently thanked Elise with a nod of her head and a look of helplessness toward Isabel Davis. That lady assumed a posture of confidence in the birthing process as she set the chloroform on the only table in the room. Seeing a peafowl fly brush nearby, she began fanning her patient.

"You need to push, Sybil," Isabel Davis instructed, adding, "Are you pushing? You have to push hard!"

"I'm trying…God knows I'm trying," Sybil Adams said, panting breathlessly. Elise noticed that she seemed more relaxed, now that someone who had experienced childbirth was there to help her.

"Where are my girls?" she asked, breathing short breaths with her mouth open.

"Aunt Celia has them. They were asleep when I left them," Elise said.

"Thank you…Lord have mercy!" she whispered with her eyes shut as pain wracked her body. With her body heaving in the throes of childbirth, she gave a final push, trying hard to stifle a scream as her baby emerged from her body to the cot. Isabel Davis went to work, first pushing away the sheet from the baby boy who began to cry weakly.

It was then that Elise realized that Isabel Davis hadn't had time to administer the chloroform, or she delayed using it because of its possible danger to the baby or the mother. The baby had come too fast, once they reached the Adams' cave. She and Drusie turned their heads as Isabel Davis wet a cloth and wiped away the birthing residue from the newborn who made low, mewing sounds. She also cleaned the mother, as best she could. She then picked up the baby and placed him on the chest of his mother.

"He seems a little slow to cry," she said, "but you've got a fine baby boy. Now, where are your scissors? We'll need to cut the cord in a few minutes."

"Look in the drawer under the table," Sybil Adams said in an exhausted but relieved voice, pointing toward the only table in the room.

As Isabel Davis looked for the scissors, Elise helped her, noticing the blood still pumping on the baby's side of the placenta. Isabel Davis wiped the scissors with a wet cloth and waited for the placenta to stop pulsating before cutting it and separating the baby from his mother. She then tied it, so that more blood wasn't lost. Then, she said, they would wait on the afterbirth which should come within maybe thirty minutes.

While they waited to see what was needed, Isabel Davis picked up the tiny baby again and placed him at his mother's breast. She then pulled up the sheet over the mother and baby, and though it was bloody from the childbirth, it provided some privacy for Mrs. Adams and her little one. Sybil Adams said that she was afraid she didn't have any milk since she hadn't had enough food to eat. Elise feared for not only her baby but for all of the babies born during the siege, since their mothers did not ingest enough food to provide milk for their offspring. When the baby finally succeeded in his quest for his mother's milk, Elise saw tears of joy come to Sybil Adams' eyes when she realized that she had milk, after all, for her baby.

Elise never knew what made her think of the tiny bird while they all stood around, trying to give the new mother support, but she looked around the small cave room and didn't see it anywhere.

"You are looking for Twiggy, aren't you?" Sybil Adams said softly. Before Elise could answer, Sybil told her with tears in her eyes that the tiny bird provided the girls' supper several evenings after Elise had brought it to them. Elise looked away from her, hoping she wouldn't shed tears, also. It was fitting that the little bird had provided nourishment for someone, as its final calling.

"They never knew," Sybil Adams said with a sigh as she looked down at her new baby.

"It was fitting," Elise said. After this, Elise motioned to Drusie and they told the new mother goodbye, that she was in the capable hands of Isabel Davis, and she should send word if they were needed again. Sybil Adams thanked them profusely for seeing about her. Isabel Davis said that she would probably stay with her new patient through the night and maybe even the next day. She wanted Drusie to come and check on her and the new mother and baby when morning came.

Leaving her lantern, Elise searched for the candle and match in her pocket, which she lit to find their way through the dark halls of the cave hallway back to the Holmes' cave, where they sat together in the main room of the dugout, glad for a time to talk. Her aunt and the Adams girls slept on, and Elise almost envied their respite from the horrors of the day-to-day siege of the city. Lighting another candle to dispel the darkness of the cave, she looked at Drusie, noticing her thinness. They spoke in low tones, trying not to waken others who shared their cave.

"I have some apples, Drusie. They're not quite ripe but

when you're hungry, they taste okay." Elise took a yellow June apple from the small bowl on the nearby table and handed it to her friend.

"Thanks...where did you find these?"

"Stone Jackson sent them to us by a courier," Elise said.

"Oh," Drusie said, taking a bite of the apple. "I didn't know whether you two were still seeing each other. I'm sure that courting is difficult when a siege is going on," she said ruefully, attempting a smile. "Oh," she said more loudly, "I have meant to tell you since the ball that Tommy thinks you are the most beautiful woman in the world. I believe he would have pursued you after the ball, if I hadn't given him a stern talking-to. I'm sure you remember that he couldn't take his eyes off you when we saw you the day after you came to Vicksburg...when we were looking at our caves. Then, he filled up your dance card at the ball. I knew you weren't interested in a boy younger than yourself, especially when you chose Stone Jackson to dance the mirror dance with you. I felt that Tommy needed someone to tell him that you weren't interested in him."

"I guess I was surprised that Tommy was almost a man after three years' time, but I have to confess that I felt flattered to have him be so sweet to me."

Elise desperately wanted to bare her heart to her friend. She wanted to tell her about her wedding plans. What would Drusie think? However, something like an invisible hand held her back. Drusie kept talking in between bites of her apple, and Elise could tell that her friend was literally starved as she relished the unripe fruit. Also, Elise was dismayed about the news that Drusie divulged.

"Do you remember Rhoda Stewart at the ball several weeks ago?" Drusie asked.

"Yes," Elise said, adding, "Actually, I remember her dress more than I remember her. She had on one of the prettiest ballroom gowns I've ever seen. Also, as I remember, she was quite a dancer."

"Oh, yes, she was," Drusie said, slightly rolling her eyes. "She even went over to Stone Jackson after you and your aunt and uncle left, and asked him to dance with her. The girl is bold, I tell you!" Before Elise could comment, Drusie talked on, and Elise wanted to hear every word she said.

"Actually, Elise, Stone Jackson was at the ball before this last one, when it ended early because the Feds decided to run the blockade that evening. It was held several weeks before you came to Vicksburg. Anyway, Rhoda asked him to dance at that ball and he agreed to. However, he didn't dance with her at this last one, though several at the party said they heard her ask him. She also told at least three people at the ball that evening that she was setting her cap for him."

At this, Elise interjected, "She what?"

"Yes, that's what she said," Drusie said, with her eyes flashing. "Oh!" Drusie continued, "What do you think about this? One of the girls who volunteers to nurse the northern soldiers at the Duff-Green House, or hospital now, where your mother is still a patient, has fallen in love with one of the enemy soldiers. They're even talking about getting married when the war is over. Now, just what do you think about that?" Drusie crossed her arms over her chest and threw her head back as if to give her question more emphasis.

"I think it's awful! They're killing our soldiers and are trying to kill us!" Elise said.

"Well, she's not the only one. I've heard of others who are falling for the northern soldiers. I guess those boys have meat on their bones and pretty blue uniforms with shiny brass buttons. Compared to our barefooted, half-starved boys in too-short uniforms which were boiled to rid them of vermin, and this caused them to shrink – well, you get the picture, Elise. They're nursing them back to health in the hospitals and the northern soldiers are falling for the southern girls, too, I've been told."

"But how could they sell out our soldiers who are fighting for us? I've volunteered to help in our hospitals, but I certainly wouldn't set my cap, as you said, for someone who is trying to kill us!" Elise said vehemently.

"Another thing I've heard," Drusie said, lowering her voice to a whisper, "I've heard through the grapevine that the girls in the bordello on the river are having their own ball, since they weren't invited to ours several weeks ago. I've also heard that some of the northern soldiers have gotten word of it and plan to attend. They're even going to ease up on their missiles so their boys can make it across the ravines and the river and go to the ball."

"Well, I hope our boys have better sense than to attend such a thing!" Elise cried out, horrified. She then remembered hearing the soldier on the train whispering to Jack about the bordello. It was only a few weeks past, but it seemed like a long time ago.

"I've heard that some plan to go," Drusie said, adding, "You'd think they'd leave those girls alone, what with the diseases they're giving to the soldiers that visit them."

"I agree," Elise said, before changing the subject, "Oh, I meant to ask you, Drusie, did you and Mrs. Isabel see the petition going around, asking people to sign it if they wanted General Pemberton to grant a flag of truce to send the women and children beyond the lines?"

"We saw it, all right, and passed it on. No one had signed it when it came to us. General Pemberton said he could not do it for one person, but if a majority of the citizens of Vicksburg signed it, he would do so. When we saw the petition, no one had signed it, except the three people who had gotten it up! We all were sufficiently warned. I'm not going anywhere," she sniffed, holding her nose in the air and taking a last bite of her apple.

"Well, when we saw it, no one had signed, either, except the three people you mentioned. No, we aren't leaving, either. We will all stick together…and die together, if need be."

Both friends looked at the floor of the cave, and when they looked at each other, their eyes were brimming with tears. Drusie spoke first, saying that she was going on back to her family's cave. If Mrs. Adams needed her or her mother anymore, she could let them know.

"Well, remember, Drusie," Elise said, "your mother wants you to check on her and Mrs. Adams and the new baby in the morning. Of course, I'll be checking on them, too."

"I will. I'm glad we had this time to talk, Elise. It's a wonder we're all still alive."

Elise hugged her friend, agreeing that it was good, being able to talk to each other again. Elise wanted to tell her of all that she and Stone were planning, once the war was over, but something told her to keep it a secret until…until when, she didn't know. She only knew that Drusie's friendship was enduring and cherished, and she prayed they would both be alive at the end of the war.

"Elise, I wish the best for you and Stone. When you even mentioned his name, I could tell that you were in love with him. I'm just so sorry that you both can't have a normal and happy courtship without bullets and missiles flying around."

Elise was taken aback by her friend's words. She had no idea that her face and words betrayed her when she even said Stone's name. She wanted to confide in Drusie that Stone had asked her to marry him, but again something restrained her. She smiled and tried to act nonchalant when she spoke again.

"He's been so good to my family and me, how could I not like him, Drusie," she said.

"I know it's more than that, Elise, and when the time is right, you'll let me know all about it," Drusie said with a smile.

"Bye, dear friend," she said as she left the cave.

~ O ~

It was long past the time for another get-together at the Holmes' cave, so after the invitation was issued, those in nearby dugouts made their way through the murky corridors of the caves to the Holmes' cave. As usual, some brought their own chairs and newspapers and musical instruments, along with a few pets which had, so far, survived the siege. Celia Holmes welcomed their neighbors as Elise lit candles and lanterns.

As everyone settled down and someone opened the assembly with prayer, at the request of Celia Holmes, Isabel Davis held up a letter which she had recently received. She said the letter had survived a trip down the Yazoo and Mississippi rivers by a daring and secret courier who defied the dangerous Union gunboats by gliding past them under cover of darkness, holding onto a log. The splotched ink on the tattered envelope testified to the letter's encounter with dirty water and the tight clutch of the courier.

"I won't read the letter, but I'll tell you what my friend and others like her, whose homes are in the midst of Yankee headquarters, are going through. She says in her letter that one morning some of Grant's men came and asked her father if he'd seen any "Rebs," as they call our men. Her father said he hadn't seen any, so they rode on, only to be ambushed by our soldiers in some gullies near their house. Several of the Federals were killed and others were wounded. These were brought into my friend's home until an ambulance came from their base near the Big Black River. Well, the Yanks were furious and accused my friend's father of knowing about our soldiers, which of course was untrue.

"When the dead and wounded were removed from their home, the Yanks told my friend's father that they would kill him if he was still at his home that evening. He had to leave without anything, only the clothes on his back, and couldn't take anything from their home. Everything on the property was burned, including the outhouses and chicken coops."

Shadows played on the clay walls of the cave as Isabel Davis continued to reveal the contents of the letter, which gave those in the caves information about what was going on in other parts of their state. The letter even made the listeners appreciate the fact that the enemy hadn't gotten to them yet and that they had a place of refuge in their caves. Everyone had engrossed expressions on their faces as Isabel Davis continued.

"The bushwhackers took everything from my friend's grandfather, but they left the hogs in the woods, so these provided the only food left for the family. The Yanks burned her grandfather's gin house where he had stored cotton from three years' pickings. However, after this, two men in her family took long poles with forks on the ends and pulled out eighteen bales of the burning cotton. Then, they took the bales to the nearby creek and later hid them in the woods. As they faced near starvation, two of the old men took one bale of the cotton on an old cart they found and pulled it to the Yankee camp, where they sold it for a good bit of money.

"Well, they took the money and stashed it in a hidden drawer in my friend's grandmother's dresser. That night, two men who had seen her grandfather get the money came to his house and put a pistol to his head, demanding the money. Her grandmother was quick thinking, though, because she gave the men rolls of Confederate money in her wardrobe. She knew it was worthless, but obviously they did not, as they did not return to their home."

At this revelation, everyone in the cave laughed and clapped their hands at the grandmother's ingenuity. Elise marveled at the grit and determination of those who had found ways to cope with their adversities. She and the others listened with fascination as Isabel Davis told of other episodes written about in the letter.

"Obviously, my friend's grandmother is a resourceful person. She put some hams between two mattresses on her bed and asked one of my friends to lie on the bed and pretend she was ill. My friend said she stood by her with a fan which she waved vigorously over the 'patient' whenever a Yankee entered the room." Everyone in the cave room smiled at this.

Isabel Davis continued telling about the contents of the letter. "I don't know whether you have heard that the camel 'Old Douglas,' which had been adopted by the 1st Missouri Brigade was killed by a Federal sharpshooter. It seems the Missourians were treated to camel steaks after this happened. No word on how the meat tasted, but when you're starving, it seems that anything is good." No one offered any comments about the luckless animal, but Elise remembered seeing the camel the first morning of her return to Vicksburg, when Scipio drove her and her aunt to Sky Parlor Hill. It seemed like ages ago, but only a few months had passed. For some reason, the unheralded demise of the camel brought tears to her eyes.

Isabel drew from her pocket a piece of paper which she held up for all in the cave to see.

"This was in one of the balloons that were shot down by our sharpshooters. We think it's just more propaganda from the Feds. It's titled 'To Our Friends in Vicksburg.'" Everyone in the cave urged her to read it.

"Cave in boys and save your lives, which are considered of no value by your officers. There is no hope of relief for you. Sherman with 60,000 men is chasing Joe Johnston. Grant with 90,000 men environs Vicksburg. You can't escape in those boats, that game is blocked on you. The 12,300 men under McCulloch, on whom you depended to help you out, are retreating back to Harrisburg, well whipped, even Colonel H., who hopes to escape in his fast six (6)-oared whale boat, can't come in. Not one soldier of you will be heard of, as connected with the siege of Vicksburg, while your officers will all be spoken of as heroes. Your present form of Government crushes out the hopes of every poor man, distinction is kept for the aristocracy of the South. You have better friends on this side than on that, the friends of freedom." It was signed "LIBERTY."

As everyone looked at one another, obviously wondering whether the flyer had any truth in it, someone else held up an anonymous note to General Pemberton, which was circulating throughout the army and also the residents of Vicksburg. The man who had lost an arm and a leg in the war, and who held onto a crutch, nevertheless stood up to read the ragged page, as if to magnify its meaning. Someone else held a candle for him to see, as he read:

"Sir: In accordance with my own feelings, and that of my fellow-soldiers with whom I have conferred, I submit to your serious consideration the following note:

We as an army have as much confidence in you as a commanding general as we perhaps ought to have. We believe you have displayed as much generalship as any other man could have done under similar circumstances. We give you great credit for the stern patriotism you have evinced in the defense of Vicksburg during a protracted and unparalleled siege.

I also feel proud of the gallant conduct of the soldiers under your command in repulsing the enemy at every assault, and bearing with patient endurance all the privations and hardships incident to a siege of forty-odd days' duration.

Everybody admits that we all covered ourselves in glory, but alas! General, a crisis has arrived in the midst of our siege.

Our rations have been cut down to one biscuit and a small bit of bacon per day, not enough scarcely to keep soul and body together, much less to stand the hardships we are called upon to stand.

We are actually on sufferance, and the consequence is, as far as I can hear, there is complaining and general dissatisfaction throughout our lines.

We are, and have been, kept close in the trenches day and night, not allowed to forage any at all, and, even if permitted, there is nothing to be had among the citizens.

Men don't want to starve, and don't intend to, but they call upon you for justice, if the commissary department can give it; if it can't, you must adopt some means to relieve us very soon. The emergency of the case demands prompt and decided action on your part.

If you can't feed us, you had better surrender us, horrible as the idea is, than suffer this noble army to disgrace themselves by desertion. I tell you plainly, men are not going to lie here and perish, if they do love their country dearly. Self-preservation is the first law of nature, and hunger will compel a man to do almost anything.

You had better heed a warning voice, though it is the voice of a private soldier.

This army is now ripe for mutiny, unless it can be fed.

Just think of one small biscuit and one or two mouthfuls of bacon per day. General, please direct your inquiries in the proper channel, and see if I have not stated stubborn facts, which had better be heeded before we are disgraced.

From—MANY SOLDIERS"

The cave room was silent as everyone lowered their heads, obviously feeling the same as the "many soldiers" who had anonymously signed the letter which bespoke of desperation. Finally, one of the musicians in attendance brought out his fiddle and began playing a frenetic version of "Dixie." This brought about singing and clapping and a contrived relief among the group.

After the passing of several days, a lull from the enemy's shelling gave Elise the opportunity to climb the hill above the cave to her aunt's house. Her aunt was visiting Sybil Adams and her new baby whom she named "Vick," a shortened version of her husband's name, "Victor." She told them that the name also stood for "victory," which she hoped the South would have.

Elise was almost desperate to see Stone again, to be held by him and to hear him say that he loved her. Her heart ached for him. She hoped that maybe he would drop by her aunt's house, as he had done before.

The back-porch door hung open, and Elise could only hope that the cover was still over the cistern. She knew that soldiers often drank from the cistern on the back porch and even filled jugs with water from the cistern to take back to the trenches. In their haste, they had probably left the porch door open, but she was thankful to see the cover in place over the cistern. Fresh water was a precious commodity for everyone in the war-ravaged city. She had witnessed barrels of water brought from the river for the soldiers and by teamsters to water their stock. They had to brave fire from federal sharpshooters across the river each time they filled their barrels. She remembered the bloated bodies of dead horses and mules in the water that their soldiers drank.

She was thankful, also, that soldiers didn't occupy the house and grounds, as they did other homes, since her aunt's house was farther away from the batteries. Elise washed her face and hands and was about to proceed further, with an all-over bath, when she heard the front door of the house open. Hoping the visitor was Stone, she was walking to the parlor when she heard her brother, Jack, calling for her.

"Sister?" he said, loudly.

"I'm here, Jack," Elise said as she entered the parlor. She was surprised to see the hurried and worried look on her brother's face.

"What's wrong, Jack?" she asked.

"I want to show you something, Elise," he said. "I didn't find you in the cave, so I figured you'd be up here," he added.

"Well, what is it?" she asked.

"Never mind. I want you to see something, but we're going to need to go through some dense woods and you'll need to put on some of my clothes, because there'll likely be brambles and underbrush." Jack was spitting out his words in a voice she'd never heard him use. He was obviously upset about something.

"Where are we going, Jack?"

"You'll see. We're going toward Grant's redan or redoubt or camp. I get all of those military structures mixed up, but it's where Grant has his headquarters, almost directly across from us. It's probably less than a mile from here."

"But, Jack, that's dangerous! Why in the world are you subjecting both of us to not only the bullets but also the tangled underbrush. There'll be briers and snakes and…no, I don't want to go!"

"Elise, it's very important that you go. You'll be glad you went. It won't take long. You'll need to wear some of my clothes, though. You can't go in your dress." Elise looked at him, unbelievingly.

"I can't believe this! Whatever can be so important for me to see that you'd risk both of our lives?" she asked. She stared at Jack, and something about the tiredness in his eyes, indeed his posture and his words, made her realize that what he wanted her to see was of vital importance.

"All right, Jack, I'll go," she said in a wondering and somewhat frightened voice.

"Good! Now go to my room and try to find some of my old shirts and pants...get the older ones...they're smaller...and meet me back here in the parlor as soon as you can. It's early and they aren't shelling us yet," Jack said, adding, "Please hurry, Sis!"

Elise hurried as best she could up the stairs, holding up her dress and petticoat. She rushed to Jack's room and looked through his clothes that were left in the wardrobe. Finding the smallest looking shirt and pants, she put them on. She rolled up the bottom of the pants and found a sash from her room to hold up the pants. She knew she looked like a fright, but didn't everybody in Vicksburg? She balled up her hair and put a floppy hat of Jack's on her head, and she was ready for whatever farfetched escapade her brother had in mind.

She thought Jack would laugh when he saw her, but she was mistaken. He even seemed more grim. What in the world did he want her to see? All she could do was trust him.

"I'm ready," she said, eyeing him closely.

"Come on. Let's go!" he said. She followed him out the back door, praying that the shelling of the town would be delayed. They climbed down the lengthy strata of caves, then began climbing up the next hill that was covered with magnificent magnolia trees in full bloom and dense undergrowth. However, a path of sorts led through the woods, and Jack stayed on the rough path. They followed the hilly lay of the land, going up and down the steep slopes, with Jack motioning to her with his finger to his lips to be quiet. After what Elise perceived to be maybe a mile, Jack looked back at her and whispered a few words.

"We're almost close enough now. There'll be several tents there. As I was told it, Grant was staying in a nice house there, but they needed wood, as I have heard, to build their gabions and for other uses, so he let his soldiers tear down the house for the wood. Shh...I don't want them to hear us. Ahead is Grant's camp. It's his headquarters, I guess. He's usually where you can see him, I've been told, and sometimes he isn't even in uniform. Just follow me and we've got to be quiet," he whispered.

Elise had never particularly wanted to see General Grant, but now she was surprised that she was actually wanting to see the northern general, called by some "Unconditional Surrender" Grant. She followed along behind her brother, wondering why he would want to risk their lives, creeping toward the northern army.

Suddenly, Jack halted, and they both could hear men talking. Slowly and quietly, Jack began moving again, bent over but with his eyes glued ahead. Elise tried to walk silently, also. Presently, they could see blue-coated soldiers moving around beyond the low parapet ahead of them. The white tents were visible, also. The parapet was being reinforced with bullet-proof sandbags, placed far enough apart to leave loopholes for musketry and logs. Some of the soldiers appeared to be drinking their morning coffee, and the powerful aroma of it, borne on the slight breeze that carried it to the thicket where Elise and her brother waited, reminded Elise that she hadn't enjoyed a cup of coffee for a number of weeks, except the dried sweet potato coffee that they all had learned to drink in Vicksburg.

Elise noticed four of the soldiers playing the card game, euchre, while another group was playing "seven-up" under a blanket spread over the hammers of muskets driven into the ground. This gave them a shadowy relief from the sun that bore down relentlessly. The games continued even as Confederate shells burst over them.

On a tall tree stump, a bald eagle surveyed the land, its wings spread and its white head moving majestically from left to right. Elise had heard of the eagle…she remembered that someone dubbed it "Old Abe," after the president, though the Rebel soldiers and the citizenry of Vicksburg dubbed it "that Yankee buzzard."

She had heard that it was the Union mascot. She had also heard that when the top generals passed by the bird, they would raise their hats. This would elicit a cheer from the Yankee soldiers, and the eagle would spread its large wings.

Some of the southern soldiers vowed they'd rather capture or kill the eagle than many Federal soldiers. As some of the Confederate weapons roared over their heads, the bird suddenly lifted its wings and flew from the stump toward Jack and Elise, causing Elise to jump, before it veered away and swiftly soared back to its stump. Elise wondered whether the bird knew, somehow, that they were there in the tangle of large trees and undergrowth.

Jack slowly looked back at Elise, with his forefinger to his pursed lips, and told her to look at the man in the nearest tent, getting up from a small table where another man sat, along with a boy of maybe ten or twelve years of age. The man rising from the table was dressed in rumpled, nondescript civilian clothes.

"That's Grant," Jack whispered, "and the boy is his son." As Elise peered through the thicket of trees, her heart sank within her when the other man at the table rose and walked over to Grant. She nearly fainted when she realized the man was Stone Jackson!

An involuntary sob sounded in her throat, causing Jack to put his finger to his lips again. His eyes were looking into her own now, wanting her to see what he had brought her to see. The shock was almost too much for Elise to bear. She wanted to scream out that it wasn't really Stone. Now, she knew why her brother had insisted that she go with him. She would never have believed it, if she hadn't seen him with her own eyes.

She felt like the breath had been knocked out of her. She couldn't think. She was torn between disbelief and horrified acceptance. What was he doing consorting with the enemy? She wanted to cry, needed to cry, but not in front of her brother. She felt like a fool.

"Jack, what is he…a…a spy?" she whispered, her voice trembling.

"Looks like it," he said.

"Let's go back. I mustn't see him again," Elise whispered, and she turned her head, so her brother wouldn't see the tears gushing from her eyes and cascading down her cheeks.

"Yes, we need to get back before the shelling starts again," Jack said, now leading the way back to the cave. Elise waited to talk again until they were nearly back to the cave. She dried her tears with the ends of her sash before speaking again.

"Jack, thank you for showing me something that I doubt I would have believed, if I hadn't seen it with my own eyes. Please…let's don't mention this to anyone else in the family, especially Mama and Aunt Celia. Stone may be a spy, but he has literally kept us alive, Jack. He used to bring us food, himself, but now he has a courier to bring it to us." The tears kept coming, and she kept drying her face with the damp sash.

"I agree. I know it upset you, Sis, but I had to let you know. I know he's brought food to you and Aunt Sissy and also to Mama and Uncle Alan and myself," Jack said, looking away with his head down. When he raised his head and turned toward her, she saw that his eyes were also filled with tears. Quickly, he again followed the rough path back to the Holmes' cave, motioning for Elise to follow him. When they came out of the woods, Jack said a quick goodbye and told Elise to be careful, before setting out for the trenches.

Elise climbed back up the embankment to her aunt's home, glad to have some time to herself before facing her aunt again in their cave. She didn't intend to tell anyone else in the family what she had found out about Stone Jackson. After entering the house, she went back upstairs and took off Jack's clothes which, she noticed, were covered with beggar's lice. At that moment, she didn't care whether she lived or died. She went across the hall and threw herself on her bed, sobbing, until she finally slept.

Chapter Eight

Elise kept the terrible secret that Jack had revealed to her in her heart, refusing to divulge it to anyone. Mechanically, she faced each day, trying to find enough to eat for herself and her aunt. She knew that her beloved aunt suspected something, but she had ceased asking Elise what had happened to trouble her so. Elise knew that the change in her demeanor was affecting everyone around her, but she couldn't make the grieving ache go away. It was as if Stone had died.

She never wanted to see him again. She couldn't bear it. Yet, she yearned to hear what he would say, if they should see each other again. However, she felt that no explanation could possibly suffice. He was a traitor. He was aiding and abetting the enemy…the enemy which destroyed her father's leg and foot and hurt her mother, so that she remained in the hospital.

As the siege intensified, Elise found herself drawn to her room and her bed in her aunt's home above the cave. Since falling asleep in her bed after finding out the truth about Stone Jackson, she realized how comfortable her bed was, compared to the lumpy cot in the cave. When she mentioned this to her Aunt Celia, she was surprised by her answer which she gave in the midst of a coughing spell.

"Elise, I really don't think we're getting as much shelling here now, as the rest of the town is suffering. If you want to take a nap in your room, or even spend the night, rather than this damp dugout, then do what you want to do. I've been worried about you, Elise. I know that something other than this siege has been troubling you, and I know that when you think it's the time to tell me, you will. You know that I love you like my own daughter."

"I love you, too, Aunt Celia. We're all trying to survive this war in many similar ways but also in different ways. Aunt Celia, I've grown up so much in such a short length of time. I was only a spoiled, fun-loving girl when I arrived here on the train just a few weeks ago. I feel as though I've lived a lifetime now, and I've seen so much. Sometimes, it's all hard to bear. Please forgive me for complaining. I know we are blessed. You and Mama and Jack and Uncle Alan…we're still alive! Yes, Mama was injured, but she's going to be fine. Oh, Aunt Celia, I love you!" Elise hugged her aunt who kissed her on her cheek.

"I'm going up to the house. I may spend the night there, too, Aunt Celia, and I'll bring water back with me when I come back to the cave."

"Isabel is coming today. I'll be fine," Celia Holmes said, as Elise picked up several jugs for the water and left the cave.

The climb up the hill to her aunt's house was especially difficult, carrying the jugs and needing to touch the hilly ground, underfoot, for balance. The back door hung open again, but the cover was in place on the cistern. She left the empty jugs on the porch and latched the back door to deter any Yanks from entering. She knew it was dangerous to stay in the house, but it was equally as dangerous in the cave. She needed to be alone, to think and to ponder all that she had learned about Stone Jackson.

Once in her room, she sat in one of the silk-covered chairs and unlaced her shoes. She sat resting her elbow on the chair arm with her chin on her hand. She closed her eyes and felt Stone's presence in the room. She wondered what they would say to each other, if ever they should meet again.

Among her many diverse feelings about Stone, she also felt guilt. She, too, had been consorting with the enemy, though unknowingly. She felt violated. She was too confused and shaken and even embarrassed to tell her family. Too, Stone had brought food to all of them. He had literally kept them alive.

She remembered one of the last times she had seen him, when the cow was shot at the top of the ravine. He had hurried, on foot, to get some of the meat for her and others in their cave. Then, he had built a fire pit outside their cave and had cooked strips on it for their supper that evening. The remainder he rubbed with salt which he had brought with him (when had any of them had any salt?) and had put the meat on canes laid across frames in the pit. With a slow fire beneath it and the heat of the sun, the meat cooked while he strung cord from the logs at the roof of the cave and showed her and her aunt how to hang the jerky, once it was done. She and others in the cave had eaten it when there was nothing else to eat.

Her thoughts continued. Stone had never questioned her or her Uncle Alan about military doings. Of course, she knew nothing about such. She had wondered where he was getting the food that he brought. She remembered wondering about the salt he had used to cure the beef, when the cow was shot on the hill. No one else had salt, only saltpeter. The salt was superior to saltpeter, but she had wondered where he had gotten it.

Looking back, she had also wondered why he rarely wore a uniform. He had worn a Confederate uniform at the beginning of the siege, but after that, he began wearing civilian clothes. She remembered when he had retrieved her uncle's letter at the beginning of the siege and had brought back a letter from her father. The pieces of the real-life puzzle began to fit together, and they made her feel young and foolish.

Well, she was no longer young and foolish. The war had taken away her youth, but maybe it had given her a little wisdom. She wondered whether she looked as old as she felt.

She walked over to the mirror on the door of the armoire. Standing in front of it, she realized how thin she was. The dowdy homespun dress hung loosely from her shoulders. Heretofore, she would have put on a pretty dress, thinking that the man she loved might come and see her in the unbecoming dress she wore, but everything was different now. She didn't care how she looked, even if he should walk through the door.

"Elise?"

Elise gasped, not knowing what to do. She recognized the voice immediately.

"Elise, it's Stone." The door handle rattled and Stone Jackson entered the room.

"Elise, darling," he said, smiling and moving toward her with outstretched arms.

"Don't touch me!" Elise said in a low voice, moving away from him.

"What?" Stone's smile left his face, but he continued moving toward her as she backed away.

"You're…you're a traitor!" Elise said, continuing to back away until she touched the chair where she had been sitting. She tried her best to keep tears from coming, but they flooded her eyes, anyway.

"I saw you! You were sitting at a table at Grant's headquarters!"

Stone stepped within a few feet of Elise, his facial expression a slow contortion of mixed emotions.

"I knew this would happen, Elise. I just didn't know when. Do you know how dangerous it was for you to go through the woods to Grant's headquarters? Whoever carried you over there was risking your life and his, too. I assume Jack carried you there."

"You're right," Elise said, gaining courage to say all that needed to be said.

"I love you, Elise," Stone said as tears filled his eyes.

Again, Elise moved away.

"I've wanted to tell you everything ever since I first saw you, but I knew I'd never see you again, if I did. Please sit down, for God's sake, and let me tell you why I am here at all." Elise wiped her eyes with a hanky from her pocket and sat down, looking at the floor and refusing the handkerchief which Stone held out to her.

"When the war began," he said, swiping at the tears on his own face, "I was asked to lead one of the Union armies, but I refused because I have three brothers fighting for the South. Do you know that two brothers are fighting against each other here, in this campaign? Yes, as I understand it…one lives in the South and one lives in Indiana, I believe. Anyway, they are here, within a few yards of each other, and fighting against each other. One had even named his son after his brother…that's how close they were before the war.

I paid my money to stay out of the war. I wanted the Union to stay a union. I didn't want a divided country, and I didn't want to fight against my brothers…not only my brothers but others in my family who are fighting with the Rebels. I think they are misguided, but some actually think they're taking a stand for states' rights." Stone paused and walked over to the fireplace where he rested an arm on its mantel. When he looked at Elise, he began speaking with such passion that she gasped.

"I don't believe in slavery, Elise! Oh, I know it has existed throughout the ages, but it's not right. I couldn't fight for the South for that reason, also. I was torn between the two. As you may know, President Lincoln issued the Emancipation Proclamation in January of this year, so the slaves are free to do as they please.

Yes, I attended West Point with the knowledge that I was being trained for military leadership, but I thought it would be for possible conflict with other countries---not for an internecine war between brothers! I guess my heart is with the Confederacy, but my mind and soul are with the Union, hoping that our great country will survive and will remain undivided."

Stone began walking back and forth as he talked, and Elise found herself listening to ideas she had never considered. She had just taken slavery for granted. It had been a way of life for her family and for the South as a whole. It had never crossed her mind that the smiling, helpful slaves in her family had rather be free. Stone began talking again, sometimes looking at her and other times looking upward, as if for divine assistance.

"You may not know, Elise, that the state of Mississippi and Vicksburg, especially, did not want to secede from the Union. In 1851, a Special Convention met in Jackson and the delegates voted to remain in the Union. You see, this was ten years before the war began. You were six years old at the time, Elise. A lot happened in those ten years to persuade the state to secede from the Union, but after the state seceded, Vicksburg citizens remained loyal to the Union. The town had ties to the North and was especially connected to the Midwest because of the river. The citizens also had a genuine love for our country…undivided. Finally, however, not wanting to be isolated from the rest of their brothers in the South, they agreed to secede. I can certainly understand their sentiments, as I, too, was torn between the two."

"Also, you may not know, Elise, that your Uncle Alan was not for secession. I'm sure he was in a quandary just like me. I have felt, all along, that his heart is not in fighting in the trenches but he's carrying on, like everyone else."

Stone walked over to the window where he stood for several moments, looking at the deserted outbuildings of the Holmes' plantation. Turning around, he walked toward Elise and held out his arms, but Elise turned her head, denying him. At this, he walked back to the mantel, where he rested his arm and continued talking.

"Elise, our country was founded on ideals never known in the history of the world. Our Declaration of Independence and our Constitution are two of the greatest documents ever written. What other country guarantees to its citizens what these documents do? I love this country and I want it to survive undivided. I can understand why you feel as you do, but I think you would agree with all I have said, if you would really think things through and not believe all the rhetoric that has polarized this great nation.

"My father and the president have been friends through the years," Stone said. Elise looked at him with raised eyebrows, when he mentioned the reviled President Lincoln, and he looked away momentarily before continuing.

"You know, the President was born in Hodgenville, Kentucky, my hometown, and he lived there during his early boyhood years. His family and mine have been friends through the years, long before he became President." Stone paced the floor before continuing with his explanation of the tangled web he found himself in.

"President Lincoln asked me to come down here to check on General Grant for him. General Grant has a problem with alcohol, as you may know. Grant's son, Fred, has been with him, which I guess the president didn't know, so he's usually sober when his family is with him." Stone paused before continuing. "I didn't come as a spy, however. I'm sure General Grant knows why I came, and he knows the President sent me. He knows he has a drinking problem.

"I came down with the Army Corps of Engineers about the time the freed slaves were digging the canal through the De Soto Peninsula. General Grant asked my advice about the canal, and I told him it was a disaster. I don't know who advised him to attempt it, but it was poor advice and a lapse in judgment. I was told that 3,200 troops, mostly colored, worked on the canal, and after its failure, only 800 were left, who were fit for duty.

Now, maybe I'm bringing everything up to date, insofar as you and I are concerned." Stone smiled at Elise and for a moment she forgot that he was the enemy. Quickly recovering, she looked away, her chin in the air, still trying to stop her tears.

"Actually," Stone said, "I planned to leave the area in January, after I felt that my duty was done for the president, but maybe fate kept me here. General Grant had heard about the ball that was to be held in Vicksburg, the one before this past one …not from me, but from his spies in town. Anyway, he urged me to go to the ball and even found me a Confederate uniform to wear. He said for me to keep my eyes and ears open and to report back to him anything that would help him to end the siege of the town.

"I did not come to the area as a spy, and he knows that. He laughed and told me to go ahead and enjoy the occasion…even said I might meet a beautiful southern belle. I want him to meet you some day, Elise, to let him know that his premonition was right. Of course, that night, his boats tested the batteries all along the river, causing such a commotion that the party broke up. Well, I attended that party and when another one was held recently, I attended that one, too, still looking for this beautiful southern woman. That's when I met you, Elise, and I knew I had found her!" he exclaimed, moving toward her and holding out his arms. "I love you, Elise. Please come and let me hold you. Please don't break my heart." She saw tears in his eyes as he neared her.

"You must go, Stone! I must never see you again," Elise said, her own heart breaking.

In a low voice, he said, "Elise, I knew about Pemberton's strategy in regard to the Cincinnati, but after meeting you, I could not pass on the information to the Union generals. I never was a spy, anyway, but It nearly tore my heart out when the Cincinnati sank. I saw some of my friends drowning because they couldn't swim. I found out later that the commander of the ship couldn't swim. Imagine being in charge of a warship and not being able to swim!" Stone shook his head slowly, in amazement, his hands on his hips, looking down at the floor.

Then, looking at Elise, he said, "I'm a strong swimmer and I know I could have saved some of those who drowned. I took off my boots and was about to dive into the water when General Grant ordered me back to his headquarters. He said he couldn't risk my drowning, also." When Stone looked at Elise, she was moved again to see fresh tears in his eyes.

"I didn't give away Pemberton's plan to sink the gunboat because of you, Elise!" Having said this, Stone opened his haversack and pulled out a packet which he left on the mantel. Then, turning to Elise, he looked at her and said, "I will always love you, Elise." After this, without another glance at her, he left the room. Elise could hear his boots on the stairs and the front door closing behind him.

Elise sat for a long time in the chair, feeling like the breath had been knocked out of her. She knew that she and Jack both should tell their Uncle Alan about all they had witnessed and learned, but she hadn't seen her uncle in several weeks and it was too dangerous to make the trip to the trenches. She wondered whether Jack had told him, but she and Jack had promised not to tell anyone because Stone had brought food to all of them throughout the siege.

She looked at the bundle on the mantel, which Stone had left, and she realized how hungry she was. She walked to the mantel and could smell the ham before she opened the packet. When had she eaten ham? Its salty taste was a balm for her soul. It was still warm, as if freshly cooked. The cornbread was warm, also.

When had she eaten freshly baked cornbread? In the bottom of the packet she found several pounds of gingersnaps and butter crackers. When had she eaten such? Tears came to her eyes as she sat alone in the room, tears of appreciation for the food but also tears of grief for the love she had lost. She knew without a doubt that she would love Stone Jackson for the rest of her life.

Hearing voices outside, Elise walked over to the window and looked out. She saw several soldiers in blue uniforms, picking blackberries in her aunt's backyard near the northern end of her property. She knew that the berries were ripe and had planned to pick some for her aunt and herself. Now, she wondered whether the soldiers would leave any for her to pick. Thieving bluebellies!

After picking the berries, the soldiers scrounged around the large vegetable garden, looking for something to eat. Elise had combed the garden, herself, only a few days before, and had come up empty-handed, as she knew the soldiers would.

"Nothin' here," they called out to one another.

"What about the house?" one said, looking toward the house as Elise shrank away from the curtained window.

"Ol' Grant'll punish us, if we take anything but food, and there ain't no food in the house. I've been through it a number of times." Elise shivered at this revelation, remembering that she had locked the back door. She knew the front door was unlocked. She also knew they could force their way in, if they wanted to, but was relieved when their voices trailed away. The shelling was picking up, and she dreaded the descent to the cave, especially when she had to carry the filled jugs of water down the slippery slope and the food which she had saved for her aunt. She prayed that her Aunt Celia wouldn't notice that she had been crying.

~ O ~

Toward the end of June, Isabel and Drusie Davis appeared at the Holmes' cave with some information that the enemy was planning an especially heavy bombardment along its fifteen and a half miles of fortifications on the eastern side of Vicksburg. This would be in addition to artillery sent across the river on the western side of Vicksburg. Elise and her aunt were unsure about what to do.

Isabel Davis said she was informed that they would be safer to go across the Glass Bayou Bridge and down the road just behind their Confederate batteries. With the enemy mortars silent during the night, Elise and her aunt and the Davises and their only servant, Rufus, who had not defected to the Yankees' side, made the trip. Pitching their tent in a ravine near their soldiers' lines, they all settled down to sleep.

At daylight, it seemed that hell itself had let loose artillery so loud, they could not hear what one another said. When a cannonball came rolling into the tent, Elise and everyone in the tent fled, not knowing where to run, except back to their caves, from where they had left, trying to find a safer place. With cannon roaring from the rear and mortar booming from the river, and bullets whizzing by them, they ran for their lives. Running they did, jumping behind fences and trees and into ditches for protection, with missiles exploding above them, scattering their debris around them. Elise was praying, when she heard her aunt beside her, weeping and praying that God would save them.

Then, she saw a strange thing happen. As she looked behind them, she saw Rufus drop the tent and the large basket which impeded his running and do an about-face. He was now running toward the enemy. Elise realized then that the Davis' servant was running toward the northern army, stopping to stand behind trees as the bullets rained down on them. Elise wondered whether the Davises knew that their servant was gone.

At an ear-piercing scream of many missiles, everyone fell to the ground, only to get up and, in unison, cry out, "Run!" Only by the grace of God, they agreed with one another later, did they make it back to their caves. They found out that a woman standing outside her cave entrance had her arm torn off. They realized after this frightening and almost deadly experience that staying inside their caves was, after all, the safest place to be. The Davises were saddened but not surprised to realize that Rufus had left them.

The next day dawned with the usual sounds of musketry and artillery. Elise was glad to be back in the cave, afraid to sleep in the house since the enemy had moved closer to the town. She sat up and put on her stockings and shoes, wondering what the day would bring. Her aunt stirred on her cot, shortly opening her eyes and asking Elise what day it was.

"It's Sunday morning, Aunt Celia," Elise said as she tied her shoestrings. "I wish we could go to church," she added as her aunt pulled on her stockings and shoes. Elise drew aside the makeshift curtain, once crisp and white but now stained and soiled, and both of them were about to sit down in the main room of the cave, just as Alan Holmes and Jack entered their dugout. Elise hardly recognized her brother and uncle, for they were both emaciated and filthy. Celia reached out to hug her husband but he stepped back, urging her not to touch him.

"I'm too dirty, Celia dear, and we have vermin crawling all over us," he said tiredly. Jack, too, put out his hands at arms' length, imploring them to stay a distance away from them. Elise saw immediately that her uncle was deathly ill.

"You need a doctor, Uncle Alan," she said. "Come...sit down on the settee," she added, motioning toward the settee.

"No, I can't sit down. I'm too filthy. They tell me I have scurvy," he said, speaking slowly and wearily, bracing himself with his hand on the cave wall. "The ambulance is waiting outside to carry me to the hospital. I wanted to see you both before I go. They're taking me to the hospital at the Washington Hotel."

Weakly, he pulled his haversack over his shoulder and set it on the table in the room, along with his canteen and musket.

"I'm going with you, Alan," Celia Holmes said with a hacking, strangling cough. "Elise thinks I may have pneumonia," she added.

"You both need to see a doctor as soon as possible," Elise said as she and Jack ushered their aunt and uncle out of the cave and into the waiting ambulance. The bullets continued to fly around them as the horses pulled the ambulance away. While Elise and Jack watched from the doorway of the cave, a bullet struck the ambulance, causing the horses to snort and rear up before calming down and heading toward the hotel that now was a hospital. Once inside the cave again, Jack removed his haversack and set it on the floor of the cave.

"Look in my haversack, Elise. Mama finished making my uniform. I'm too dirty to handle it."

Elise pulled the uniform from the haversack, holding it up to inspect it. She realized that her mother had sewn all of it by hand, double-stitching the entire garment. She guessed their mother had finally come to terms with the knowledge that her son wanted to fight for the Confederacy, even if only to relay messages, and he wanted a uniform to confirm that fact. With tears in her eyes, Elise folded the homespun uniform and put it back inside the haversack. After this, she motioned for Jack to sit down, but again he refused because of his filth. They both needed to talk, something they hadn't done in weeks. It was then that Elise noticed Jack's hands which were not only dirty but also cracked and bleeding.

"Jack, what happened to your hands," she asked with a worried look on her face.

"I need some gloves. We all need gloves. General Pemberton has had us all building boats for the past few weeks."

"Boats?" she asked, puzzled.

"Boats to ferry us across the river," he said in a tired and unbelieving voice.

"What?" Elise exclaimed. "What are you talking about?" Vaguely, she remembered hearing something about boats when the letter from the overhead balloons was read during one of their cave meetings. She listened intently as Jack explained.

"Well, the General first had us all building boats to carry him and his officers across the river, so they could escape when the Yankees finally capture the city, but then no one would build any, until he agreed to ferry all of us across the river to the Louisiana side. I have needed gloves but couldn't find any. We were having to tear down houses to get the wood to build the boats. If you've made any trips into town, you may have seen them. I'm afraid the boats aren't something you could trust with your life."

"No, I haven't tried to go into town. It's dangerous just to look out the cave opening," Elise said.

"I don't know how Pemberton plans to transport thousands of people across the river. I guess each boat could make return trips, but I think the strong current would either tear them apart or push them on down the river. I don't think many people think the boats are safe to use." Elise shook her head slowly, amazed that all of this was going on while she and her aunt were buried in the cave. She had made only one trip to the house for water since the increased shelling of the city and she knew it was past time to go again. She was just so afraid to venture up the hill behind the cave to do it. As if reading her thoughts, Jack suggested that they both climb the hill to get some water. Again, tears filled her eyes as she glanced at her brother. As Jack looked down at the floor of the cave, she saw a large bug crawl out of the pocket of his dirty uniform, then buzz around in front of him.

"Dang gallinippers!" he said, swatting at it with the back of his hand. When a bug crawled across his arm, he deftly flicked it away with his fingernail.

"What would Papa think if he could see us now?" Elise asked, noting her brother's disheveled appearance and the vermin on him, before looking down at her own dirty hands and stained dress.

"Papa and the boys may be in the same situation we're in, Sis. I wonder whether we'll ever see them again," he said with his eyes still cast down to the floor of the dugout.

Starting to cry, but refraining, Elise picked up two buckets and handed them to Jack.

"Come on...let's get the water!" she said, picking up another bucket for herself to carry up the hill.

Jack held the buckets in one hand and attempted to pull Elise up the embankment with his free hand. Appreciating his help in negotiating the hill, she purposely forgot the tiny creatures that infested his clothes and clung to his hands. Though she kept tripping over her dress, they finally reached the back door which hung open, as usual. Artillery blazed above them as they entered the relative safety of the back porch. Jack immediately began filling his buckets, then turned and filled Elise's bucket with water from the cistern.

The return downhill trip to the cave was even more difficult for Elise, as Jack had his hands full with two large buckets of water. Some of the water in all three of their buckets sloshed to the ground as they stumbled and slid back to the cave. After reaching the cave, Jack placed the water buckets inside, then told Elise he was going to go back to the house and wash off before heading back to the trenches. Grabbing his haversack, he quickly pulled his uncle's haversack over his other shoulder before gripping his uncle's canteen and musket. Purposely not meeting his sister's eyes, for he knew she would protest his taking their uncle's musket, Jack left the cave. With tears in her eyes, Elise waved goodbye to him as he sprinted back up the hill. As he entered the back porch of his aunt's and uncle's home, Elise thought about the fact that neither of them had mentioned the secret they shared about Stone Jackson.

Chapter Nine

Jack entered the back porch of his aunt's and uncle's house and stripped off his clothes, glad to be ridding himself of the crawling scum that had made his life miserable in the trenches. After throwing his soiled clothes out the back door, he looked at his emaciated body, noticing the red, itchy welts that he had clawed until they bled. Some lice were still attached to his body, which he systematically picked off and threw out the back door. Fleas hopped from his legs to his arms and settled on his chest, but when he tried to catch them, they hopped away.

"Dang fleas!" he muttered out loud, pulling off the chiggers which were attached to his skin, plump with his blood. The itching they caused was almost unbearable.

He knew his head was infested, also. He found some bath cloths and towels and lye soap nearby. He could smell the perfumed soap but he wanted none of that. Good old lye soap was what a man should use, he thought, and he proceeded to bathe himself. Unzipping his haversack, he found the comb which he had used since the siege began and ran its teeth through his hair, removing more of the scaly critters which clung to the comb, all of them alive and fat with his blood. With disgust, he stood on the back steps naked, with the screen door providing a shield of sorts and peeled the critters from the comb. He did this until the combing produced no more crawly tormentors.

Jack washed himself all over, including his hair. He then washed his comb and put it back in his haversack. After drying himself with a towel he found near the cistern, he reached again in his haversack and pulled out the uniform which his mother had made for him. When he pulled on the pants, he was at first dismayed to find the drawstring at the waist, but then he realized it was necessary to hold up the pants. His mother knew that his weight loss would preclude using his belt.

He tied the drawstring, then put on the shirt which buttoned down the front, covering the tied drawstring. The shirt was too large, but his mother had done the best she could, and he was proud to have a new and clean uniform. Last of all, he pulled out the gray slouch hat with the red feather and placed it on his head. Next to his new uniform, it was his pride and joy, even though a Yank had given it to him!

Jack hurried back to the trenches, dodging the missiles and bullets that whizzed over him and dreading the muck and mire he'd be dealing with in his new uniform. At least he was free, for a while anyway, from the wretched vermin that attacked all of the soldiers in the trenches. Upon reaching his regiment, he was handed a spade and pick and told to dig in the saps which were slowly working their way toward Grant's army. Confederate sharpshooters manned guns mounted at rifle pits on their parapet. As bullets from the enemy peppered the Rebel fort, the soldiers on both sides dug their trenches and tunnels toward each other.

When Jack commenced digging, he was glad he didn't have to sit in the trenches on the riverfront. That's where the festering crawlers were, though the mosquitoes plagued all of the men as they dug the saps on the eastern side of the town. They were only a few hundred yards from the Yanks, he guessed.

The strains of "Dixie" filled the air as the Rebels dug out the hilltops, attempting to make ditches with sides tall enough for soldiers to stand up in them. As the soldiers heard the music, first one, then several began singing the words and somehow the digging went faster. As the music died down, the Rebels heard a musical reply from the northern trenches when "Hail Columbia" drifted across the hills and ravines and into the ditches they were digging.

Suddenly, Jack felt a hand on his shoulder, and he was surprised to see the grinning face of his friend, Tommy Davis, who stood, stooped over, beside him.

"How's it going, Jack?" he asked.

"It's slow," Jack said, grinning back and adding, "We have to bend over to dig, and we can't straighten up because the sides aren't tall enough yet. We'll have our heads blown away, if we stand up."

"Yeah, well, this must be your first day sapping. I've been digging probably a week now, here on the east side. I wanted to do it, and Papa let me…better than dying a slow death in the river trenches."

"Where is Mr. Davis?" Jack asked.

"He left yesterday…an ambulance took him to one of the hospitals…had dysentery something awful and nowhere to go. I sent a courier to let Mama and Drusie know, but I don't know which hospital they took him to."

"I'm sorry about your father, Tommy," Jack said, adding, "Hey…looks like you've got on a new uniform, too…did Mrs. Isabel make it for you?"

"She did. It's already dirty, though no way to keep it clean." The reunited friends were startled when one of the officers in the trench began yelling at them.

"Hey…you two! We have work to do…no talking…just dig!" The officer threw Tommy a shovel and pick which Tommy managed to catch in both hands. Without another word, he began digging in earnest, attempting to make the trench deeper, so they could stand up and straighten their stiff backs. Jack had so much he wanted to say to Tommy, but it would have to be later. Right now, there was work to do, and he rose to the task.

As they kept digging, Jack realized they were connecting the separate forts with trenches and strategically placed rifle pits. In some places, the gun pits were being reinforced with wooden stockade walls. Protrusions from the walls gave them better places for firing their weapons. In front of some of these were two-to-eight-feet long, sharpened stakes in the ground, facing the enemy, with woven telegraph wire to trip any attackers.

"Pst…pst…" It was Tommy, attempting to get Jack's attention. They both looked at the officer who had reprimanded them only minutes before, but his back was to them now, as he shoveled up ahead. Jack looked at Tommy with a questioning look on his face.

"What is it?" he whispered.

"Have you heard about the Yankee guy they call 'Coonskin'?" Tommy muttered under his breath. When Jack shook his head, Tommy continued in a whisper.

"Well, they say he loads himself up with provisions and creeps close to our lines at night. He makes himself a burrow of sorts with a peephole, where he can snipe at us. He wears a cap of raccoon fur, so that's how he got his name. I heard Papa say that he's built a tower now…he used railroad ties from the Jackson and Vicksburg railroad to build it."

"That's the railroad we took to get here weeks ago…it seems like years ago now," Jack said. "Where is the tower?" he added.

"I don't know. If we try to look over our parapet or our trenches, we're shot at, so I'm not sure where it is. Papa said this fellow can look into our saps when he climbs up his tower."

Suddenly as they worked, the ground below them began to rumble and shake. Jack crouched down near the wall of the ditch they were digging and saw Tommy and their counterparts up ahead lose their balance and fall. A deafening explosion caused everyone in the ditch to drop their shovels and picks and to look far above them.

To Jack's horror, he saw the effects of the explosion, as dirt, mules, guns, wagons, poles, and spades shot into the air in the distance overhead. He was shocked to see an old Negro man raking the air against the sky, as he too was hurtled far above them, his face expressing his terror. Tommy edged over to Jack as the ditch they had left off digging continued to shudder and quake under their feet. They looked at each other, not knowing what to do, except wait for orders from the officers in front of them.

Midst the incessant roar of enemy artillery and shells, the officers ahead of them in the trench were receiving information from a courier who had crept toward them through the intertwining saps, literally on his hands and knees, so as not to risk being blown to pieces by the Yankee sharpshooters. One of the officers yelled out an explanation of the explosion.

"They mined under the 3rd Louisiana Redan…under Razor- back Hill…packed it with 2,200 pounds of gunpowder! Made a hole about fifty feet wide and twenty feet deep! The colored man who was blown up into the sky wasn't hurt at all. He was carried all the way over to the Yankee side! Keep digging!" he shouted over the incessant noise of the Union artillery. Hearing that some of the Union army were trapped in the ditch after the explosion, some of the Rebels grabbed artillery shells and rolled them down the embankment, bringing about sudden death and mangling of arms and legs of the enemy in the ravine below. Others grabbed their fuzed barrels of powder, which they called thunder barrels, and rolled them down to the enemy in the gully beneath them.

Jack and Tommy picked up their shovels and began digging with renewed urgency. Though he risked being reprimanded again,

Tommy talked between ragged breaths as he dug.

"Papa gave his permission for me to dig, but he didn't want me to fight. Actually, I have his rifle and his Bowie knife and I intend to use both," he said. Jack looked at his friend with disbelief, amazed that they both had the same idea in mind.

"I intend to do the same, though I haven't told anyone, except you just now." Jack said.

Without thinking, Tommy suddenly stood up to stretch his back, holding his shovel high above his head. The shovel flew from his grip in a hail of bullets from the Federal army, which also shot off his head. His body slumped to the floor of the sap.

With tears gushing from his eyes, Jack heard himself hollering with an ear-piercing shrillness that brought several sappers to his side. Hardened though they were, with death and devastation daily rituals, they nonetheless felt the pain of a boy of only a few years who had witnessed the sudden, horrifying death of his friend.

"You need to go back to your company, young man. You've done good work today," one of the soldiers said in a rough but soothing voice.

As Jack fell against the low wall of the trench, with tears rolling down his cheeks, two orderlies came with a litter and picked up Tommy's bloody body and mangled head. Jack watched mutely as the litter bearers walked, bent over, carrying his friend's body away for burial. It was the last time he would ever see his grinning face again. Jack, aching with the horror of it all and trying to muster some strength, crouched down and followed the litter bearers out of the trench. With his face wet with tears, he was more determined than ever to fight the vicious enemy!

Upon reaching the parapet, Jack learned that men heaved dirt into the crater that was left from the detonation of the mine under the 3rd Louisiana Redan, but missiles from the enemy swept away the dirt before it could be placed in position. They then tried sandbags which were torn to pieces and scattered. Finally, the men secured some tent flies and wagon covers which they loaded with dirt and pushed into place, providing a screen cover from the deadly assault of shot and shell and Minie balls. It was the deadliest fire of musketry ever witnessed by the men present. Nearly one hundred men were either killed or wounded by the explosion and subsequent fusillade.

Jack heard that ammunition was in such short supply that the soldiers were not allowed to fire back at the enemy. He also heard of three men who had recently floated on logs down the rivers, bringing over 200,000 caps for their weapons. Still, they were instructed not to return enemy fire.

Jack decided to go on to the river trenches where he had left his uncle's rifle. A frightening sense of loss, coupled with a festering rage, was all he could feel now. Whereas he had been somewhat undecided about fighting in what was probably going to be the final battle for the capture of Vicksburg, now he was raring to go into battle. However, though he had shot a muzzleloading weapon before, he wasn't exactly sure how to load it. As he ran toward the trenches, he longed for some sort of comfort. Yet, there was no one and nothing to turn to. Suddenly, he thought about a cup of coffee. Wasn't that what he'd seen other soldiers do? They'd make themselves a cup of coffee, and it helped to dull the pain and fear they were experiencing.

After reaching his company of sick and starving men, he dug in his uncle's haversack and pulled out the little paper sack of ground coffee and a tin can. As he prepared to boil some water for the coffee at the company's outdoor kitchen, the cook suddenly called out to him.

"Wait, young man…I've got just the thing you need for a good cup of coffee. Try this," he said, handing Jack a common cove oyster can with a bit of bent wire for a bale. "See," he continued, "you can hold it on a stick over the fire and avoid tipping it over."

Thanking him and taking his advice, Jack used the oyster can to fill with water from his canteen. While waiting for the water to boil, he looked over at a soldier in his underwear, who was tending a huge barrel of boiling water which contained his vermin-ridden uniform. Jack knew that the same barrel, or company kettle, was used by the cook to prepare meals for the soldiers, when it wasn't used for delousing their uniforms.

Jack remembered his first cup of coffee at his aunt's and uncle's house for breakfast the first day after his arrival from Jackson. It seemed like long ago, but it was only a few months prior. He had never drunk coffee until that morning, and he realized what he'd been missing. He'd tried drinking the sweet potato and sassafras and okra coffee, after real coffee couldn't be bought by the citizenry, but somehow, he couldn't stomach those substitutes. He wanted the real thing, and he was glad he still had some in his uncle's haversack.

The army knew its soldiers needed coffee to sustain them, he thought, as he sat down on a nearby tree stump and drank his cup of coffee, appreciating the way it soothed his nerves. Now, he had to prepare himself for what everyone said would be the final battle of the Vicksburg siege. First of all, he needed to practice loading his uncle's rifle and maybe even firing it, if he could find it. He needn't have worried about someone confiscating his uncle's weapon, as almost all of the men in the trenches were sick and unable to stand, much less fight. Jack found the gun where he had left it, leaning against one of the few trees remaining near his uncle's place in the trenches.

Jack slung the cartridge box from his shoulder to his right side before placing the butt of the rifle between his feet, holding the weapon with his left hand. Unfastening the cartridge box, he took a cartridge from the box, as he had seen his uncle and his father do many times. He tried to remember the steps to follow, as he brought the cartridge up to his mouth.

Using his teeth, he tore the paper cartridge, exposing the powder. Next, he poured the powder down the barrel of the weapon, followed by the Minie ball and paper. Removing the ramrod, he shoved it into the muzzle of the musket, pressing the cartridge into place. Then, he removed the rammer and returned it to its place on the weapon. Raising the rifle to eye-level, he half-cocked it with his right thumb. Then, retrieving a percussion cap from his cap pouch, he placed it on the cone of the gun. Again, using his right thumb, he fully cocked the weapon.

Looking for a target, he brought the butt of the rifle to his shoulder, aiming it at the Union naval fleet upriver. Shaking, he pulled the trigger, sending the bullet to Admiral Porter's warships. The recoil from the weapon almost caused him to lose his balance. Answering shots came back from the nearby enemy fleet.

Ruefully, Jack sighed, realizing how slow he had been, loading the weapon. He needed to practice loading and shooting and reloading, but this would take time and would use cartridges that were in short supply. He remembered seeing his aunt and Elise and other ladies who gathered at his aunt's home to make cartridges for the troops. They may have made the ones he had in his cartridge box. He decided to practice the loading and firing one more time, attempting to speed up the process.

His mind was troubled not only by the fresh memory of Tommy's terrible fate but also by his mother's image from several months before, begging him not to join the fight. His eyes misted as his mother's worried face lingered in his thoughts. He thought of Elise, also. He remembered the look on her face when he grabbed their uncle's musket and haversack and cartridge box. Did she suspect what he was planning to do?

He shrugged off these thoughts and practiced, once again, reloading the rifle. His life would likely depend on how quickly he could reload. After following the steps in order, he knew he was quicker this time. He aimed the gun toward the De Soto Peninsula and fired. Jack heard some commotion behind him and turned to see several officers addressing the forlorn men in the trenches.

"Our generals are asking all who are able to come and fight. The Feds have dug their way to the very outskirts of our city. Who will step forward and fight? Who?" The officers surveyed the men who sat and lay on the muddy ground in the riverfront trenches. When some managed to stand and face the officers, their thin bodies were evidence of all they had suffered during the past weeks. Nevertheless, they grabbed their muskets and other weapons and managed to walk unsteadily up the embankment to join the officers. The uniforms of the ones who still had uniforms were a butternut hue now, covered with mud and vermin. Others tried to stand, only to fall back to the ground, not having strength to continue the fight.

The officers moved above the different companies, asking those who were able to come forward. Jack noticed that the men who answered the call were looking in their haversacks and pockets for keepsakes which they would leave behind for their families, in the event they didn't survive. Just the thought of such made his stomach queasy. Was he as strong as these men? For the first time in his life, he faced the real possibility of his own death.

He thought of his father who lost his foot and part of his leg at Shiloh. Again, he thought of Tommy who had fully intended to fight. Jack squared his shoulders and dug into his haversack for anything he might want to leave for his family, if he should not survive the upcoming battle.

He withdrew the photo of his family, made on his fourteenth birthday, nearly a year before. He stared at his younger brothers and his father who smiled back at him from the daguerreotype. It seemed like years, rather than months since he had seen them. Would he ever see them again?

What about Elise and his mother and his Uncle Alan and Aunt Sissy? Tears started in his eyes again, and he couldn't stop the trembling that wouldn't go away. He searched further in his haversack and felt the watch which he had received as a gift from his mother and father on his last birthday.

He clutched the watch and the framed photo and looked around for someone who might keep them for him. Noticing a line of soldiers holding their valuables near the company kitchen, he assumed they would leave them with some of the mess-cooks. Most of the soldiers were writing instructions about their keepsakes, so the cooks would know what to do, in the event of their deaths. One wrote on a drumhead, another on a cartridge box, and some on top of a battery caisson.

Jack found some cartridge paper in his haversack and sat down on a tree stump near the mess kitchen to write his instructions. He gave his name and home address in Jackson, then included the names of his mother and sister and aunt and uncle in Vicksburg. In the event he did not survive the upcoming final battle, he asked that his watch and photo should be returned either to his mother, Abby Holmes, or to his sister, Elise Holmes. He also wrote where each of his family members in Vicksburg could be found, including his Uncle Alan and his Aunt Sissy Holmes.

As he sat on the tree stump, waiting to speak to one of the cooks, he couldn't help but notice how emaciated and dirty the soldiers were, who stood in line with their personal belongings. Some had watches and rings and photos, while others had small Bibles which they left in the care of the cooks who would not be fighting. The mess-cooks were assigned to cook, not fight, though there was precious little to cook now.

The cooks stood silent, trying to understand all they were being asked to do. Some of the soldiers took their Bibles and New Testaments and wrote messages on their front pages; others replaced them in their haversacks or unbuttoned their shirts and placed them near their hearts.

The enemy's roaring artillery abruptly became louder, indicating their sudden closer proximity to the Confederate parapets. The ragtag companies followed their officers' leads to one of the forts and to the recently enlarged saps on the eastern side of the city. Jack followed along, wondering whether he would be sent back to the riverfront batteries. However, no one appeared to notice him, and for that he was glad. He had almost hoped, at first, that he would be sent back, even to the Holmes' cave, but no one apparently considered him even worthy of being scolded for being a callow youth with little or no experience. He was on his own.

As he trudged along, his mother's worried face kept appearing in his mind, and he remembered with clarity how she had reacted when he came down the stairs at his aunt's and uncle's home, weeks before, in a Confederate uniform. She had wept and said, "Don't do this to me, son. You're too young." However, his Uncle Alan had then said he would look after him. Well, his uncle was gone now, and he was left to make his own decisions.

He thought of his father who would have to use crutches the rest of his life…and Tommy who was killed right before his eyes. Someone had to avenge these terrible events in his life, and he felt called to do it. He had tried to understand what the war was about, and he still did not fully understand. However, his father's injuries and his friend's ghastly death called for a reckoning that only he could bring about.

When the soldiers reached the parapet, Jack watched as some assumed posts as sharpshooters in the rifle pits. Others crouched down and entered the trenches to continue digging. As the enemy's sap-rollers approached the Confederates' parapet within sixty feet, some of the Rebels took pieces of portfire and stuffed them with cotton dipped into turpentine. They were then pushed into the hollows of their Minie bullets. These they fired from their large-bore muskets into the enemy's closest sap-roller, which set it on fire. This exposed the enemy sap and forced the Union to keep their sap-rollers wet and to begin new ones farther back.

When Jack was given orders to continue digging a trench, he carried his uncle's rifle and cartridge box with him, along with a shovel and pick. Laying the rifle and cartridge box aside, he began shoveling the sap to deepen it. After a short while, the backbreaking work took its toll and he returned to the parapet, where he could stand up and give his back rest.

At the fort, he saw that all of the field artillery, Parrott guns and siege pieces from the river batteries had been moved to the rear line. Ammunition was placed in protected and convenient places. Over a hundred guns were waiting to be used, he was told. Of course, the river batteries were still strong and intact, he overheard someone say, for they had kept all of their coastal guns.

He gazed down the parapet in both directions, noting the hired Negroes and their overseers, the four-mule teams and the 25 yoke of oxen, which he had heard about. These were used for hauling earth and materials. The forts were still being reinforced. Ravines in front of the forts were protected by abatis of fallen logs and trees, along with entanglements of telegraph wire. He knew that all the trees had been cut in front of the Confederate lines, the logs being rolled down into the hundred-feet deep, and steeper, embankments to the ravines below.

However, though the forts appeared to be well protected, he quickly learned to be careful while passing between the Rebel lines and other targets, such as the spaces for the Rebel sharpshooters, empty now because of no ammunition to spare. Many officers and men had already lost their lives to the Federal sharpshooters, because they had not used caution. Jack knew he had to be cautious in moving about.

Jack stood still at the parapet, absorbing the sights and sulfuric smells and the terrible tension of close warfare. Though cannon continued to boom, nonstop, and missiles flew over them from the nearby Federal army, the Confederate sharpshooters obeyed orders not to shoot. Jack wanted to practice loading his uncle's musket again, but the orders not to shoot applied to him, also. It seemed that ammunition was in short supply now. He waited to be told what to do. Two officers near him were talking and he listened.

"I'm afraid this is it, and there's not much we can do about it. Grant now has over 70,000 troops. Yes, we have the deep, rolling land in our favor, but they won't let our sharpshooters do what they're trained to do. Just not enough ammunition, it seems. Pemberton says every approach to the city is guarded by the Federals. I think it's time to end it, before any more of our men are killed or wounded."

"I agree, but our orders are to keep on digging the trenches and countermines and fighting the enemy. If we had the time and the tree trunks, we could build some coehorns like the ones the Yanks are sending over to us."

"How are they made?"

"They find some hard wood, like sweet gum, and the tree trunks are hollowed out and used as cylinders, strengthened by barrel straps, which are bored out for maybe six or twelve-pound shells. They have wreaked havoc on us! All of our logs are in the ravines, so we don't have what it takes to make them." As if they were ending their conversation, one of the officers looked at Jack.

"Hey, young fella! You're needed in the trenches. You can

leave your musket here. There should be some picks and shovels and axes in the trench over there. If not, come back here, and we'll round up some for you. We're in short supply of shovels, so if you don't find one to use, come back up here and we've got some made out of wood that some of the men made."

"All right, sir, but If it's all right with you, sir, I'll take my rifle with me."

"There's not much room in the trenches, but if you want to take it with you, that's all right by me."

"Thank you, sir," Jack said as he entered the sap.

Once inside the trench, Jack slid off his haversack and placed it and his uncle's musket near the entrance of the ditch. Other soldiers were in the sap, hacking away at the sides and bottom of the clay trench, using shovels and picks and axes and even their bayonets to enlarge the sap. They worked bent over, unable to stand erect after many long hours.

The Union soldiers were in their trenches and tunnels also, widening and deepening their approaches. Jack could hear their picks and shovels which were nearing the Confederate trenches. He could also hear their laughter and their voices, though he didn't understand what they were saying.

As the evening arrived, to Jack's amazement, the Federal soldiers in their saps called out to the Confederates, wanting to talk and to exchange items. Jack heard soldiers in the trench with him holler back to the Federals. They were wanting to dicker with them, also.

"We're putting up a white flag, so don't shoot. We've got sugar that we'll trade for coffee," one of the Confederate soldiers yelled.

Jack saw one of the men in the trench climb nearly to the top of the ridge where he hoisted up a bayonet with a gray slouch hat on top and a shirt hanging from it. When this was not shot at, several of the soldiers clambered up the embankment to the ridge above them and began bargaining with the Federals who stood on top of nearby escarpments, waving white flags. Then, the dickering began, and Jack ventured to the top of the ridge, wanting to watch the swapping that was taking place.

"You got sugar, you say, Johnny?" a bluecoat asked.

"I'll send you some, Yank, if you can send me some real, verified coffee."

"Hey, Butternut! Tired of your sweet potato coffee, huh? Or maybe the sweet potatoes are gone now? Want some real, honest to gosh coffee, huh? Here you go!" The soldier threw the bag of coffee and several Confederate soldiers jumped to catch it.

"Where's Hunchback?" one of the Rebel soldiers inquired. "Oh, you mean Grant? He's making plans to enter Vicksburg soon. He says he's going to dine in Vicksburg on the fourth of July."

"Well, he may just be wrong about that," a Confederate soldier replied, though his answer sounded hollow in Jack's mind.

"Hey, brother mine," a Yankee soldier hollered, and a Rebel soldier responded.

"I'm listening…what you got that I don't have, brother?" he asked.

"Oh, we've got plenty…looks like you've lost weight, little brother," the Yankee soldier yelled, then added, "I could use some good sugar,"

"We've got plenty of sugar. I'll send you some," a gray-clad soldier shouted. He had brought bags of sugar from the fort for just this time of day, for the swapping which went on every night, now that the two armies were so close to each other.

"How do you bluecoats like our sunny South?"

"Oh, bully! We like it so much; we wear our overcoats all day."

"Hey, Yanks, you fellas have any more Enfield rifles you

want to get rid of?"

"Sure, Rebs...lots of 'em, which we'll trade for batteries, and if you have any more howitzers you want to trade, bring 'em along." Before the Confederates could answer, one of the Federal soldiers ended the protracted conversations with an order.

"Lie down, Rebs, we're gonna shoot... Rats, to your holes!" he yelled with a caustic laugh. The real-life brother on the Yankee side shouted to his sibling on the Confederate side:

"I'm gonna blow your head off tomorrow, little brother!"

As the Confederate soldiers slid and jumped back into their trench, where they picked up their shovels and picks and began digging again, the Yankees' bullets soared fast and furious above them. Jack asked one of the soldiers in the ditch for some of the coffee that was thrown to them, and they all shared the contents of the bag, pouring it into their canteens.

As Jack picked up his shovel and began to dig again, a courier appeared in the trench with a whispered message for one of the officers in the trench, then left as quickly as he came. The officer cleared his throat and addressed the other soldiers in the sap.

"We have our orders for in the morning at first light. The Yanks are close enough now for us to use our ammunition and show those bluebellies that we know how to fight. We'll take a break now and try to get some sleep, so we'll feel like fighting in the morning. Use your haversack for a pillow...it's better than the hard ground.

Jack's hands were shaking as he lay down on the floor of the ditch and pulled his haversack under his head. He wondered how his father had felt at the battle at Shiloh. Was his father as fearful as he, himself, was? If only he'd had more practice loading the musket. He had hunted with a musket since he was a much younger boy, growing up in Jackson, but his father had always helped him with it. He'd never had an occasion to practice loading and reloading the weapon. Now, it was imperative that the gun be loaded quickly. He thought of his mother and knew she would be upset if she could see him now.

And what about Elise? What would she think? Once again, he thought of his father's foot and leg that were missing and his friend, Tommy, who was killed before his eyes. As he tried to prepare himself, mentally and emotionally, for the coming battle, he said a prayer, something he couldn't remember ever doing. As he gathered courage, he felt himself becoming stronger, and he actually looked forward to the morning when he could avenge the wounding of his father and the death of his friend. Exhausted, he finally slept.

Amid the constant cannonading from the enemy, early dawn spread over the town and crept into the trenches and tunnels, rousing the officers of all the forts along the parapets, both Confederate and Union, that arced on the eastern side of the city. The bugle call from the enemy was heard by the Rebels in the trenches, who readied their weapons for the planned attack.

Jack watched other soldiers as they soaked cotton in turpentine before stuffing it into the hollow of their Minie bullets, something he had seen them do before. Many of the Confederates began climbing up the embankments all along the lines of their forts. Reaching the ridge, some of them crouched and others stood, aiming and shooting into the enemy's forts. Suddenly, Yankees in the trenches climbed to the crests over the farther ravines, where they had hidden, and began returning fire. This was when Confederate drum and fife corps all along the connecting forts played, as one, the rousing notes of "Dixie."

Jack loaded his musket as quickly as he could and pulled on his hat. For once, he was glad that the hat was snug, almost tight on his head. Maybe he wouldn't lose it. He followed the other soldiers as they first stepped onto the ledge, or firing step, which enabled them to climb up the clay wall of the escarpment. Finally, able to see a little over the crest of the embankment, he saw many billowing U. S. flags. flying high on the steep ridges before them.

He also saw several of the Union flags waving from below the Confederate parapets, where fearless Yankee soldiers had dared to leave them, days before, and where they possibly could have lost their lives in doing so. He quickly glanced left and right, along the ridge where the Confederates stood, firing their muskets and reloading, and saw Rebel flags waving in the face of the enemy. When he crawled the last few feet onto the top of the hill, he squatted and aimed his musket at the line of blue-coated soldiers facing them.

He heard and felt bullets whizzing past him as he pulled the trigger and wondered whether the Minie ball would find its mark and kill one of the charging Yankees. The Federals who left their open ridges and slid down into the ravines were having problems with the abatis of logs and telegraph wire in the bottoms of the ravines. Jack quickly noticed other Confederates who were frantically trying to reload their weapons and was surprised that they couldn't load them much faster than he could. The roar of artillery unnerved him to the extent that he climbed back down, face forward, to the trench below him to finish loading his musket. Smoke from the fusillade now filled the ditches, making it difficult to breathe and almost impossible to see. Cotton bales between the forts had been set ablaze by musket blasts which further added to the confusion and ferocity of the fight.

As the smoke dissipated, somewhat, he found a stash of Minie balls in the connecting sap, which the Confederates had picked up from different battle sites, to be used again. Jack used his ramrod to force a round into the bore of his gun. Thusly armed, he again made the difficult climb back up the hill. As he neared the top, one of the men who had dug in the trench with him was struck by enemy fire and fell back into the ditch. Jack wavered between going down into the sap again or continuing on to the hilltop. The soldier did not appear to be badly injured, only dazed by the shot which knocked him off his feet. He was climbing back up to the crest of the hill, as Jack crouched on the ridge and sent a bullet into the Union soldiers who continued to fire, as others were reloading their weapons.

As Jack moved forward and felt in his pocket for a cartridge to reload his musket, the weapon was hit by enemy fire and flew from his hands, the reverberation knocking him into the ravine below. Frightened, he crawled around on his hands and knees, trying to find a place to hide among the logs and telegraph wire which filled the wide ditch. He quickly glanced at the ridge above him where several Union soldiers were attempting to reload their weapons, while being fired upon by the Confederates.

Jack noticed a log that was raised at an angle in the sap, and he quickly slid under it, hoping it would provide protection from the enemy's bullets. He could peer up through the logs now and could see the Yankees as they finished loading their muskets. They looked over into the ravine and he felt certain they were looking for him. He eased his head back under the log, hoping that he could not be seen by the soldiers in blue above him. His right foot was hurting terribly.

The battle raged on, and Jack tried not to move at all under the protecting log. Once, a Yankee soldier shot down into the ditch and Jack was certain that the Minie ball hit the log above him. He cried out, unintentionally, and was thankful that he couldn't be heard over the artillery from both sides.

Midst the hail of bullets and cannonades, Jack heard drum rolls and then the voices of many Union men in the trenches, singing "We Are Coming Father Abraham," as though they had practiced singing the song in unison before the battle. At first, Jack thought the song was about the Abraham of the Bible, but after hearing the words clearly, he realized that they referred to President Abraham Lincoln. He lay there and listened, trying to decide what to do.

> "We are coming, Father Abraham,
> three hundred thousand more
> From Mississippi's winding stream
> and from New England's shore
> We leave our plows and workshops,
> our wives and children dear
> With hearts too full for utterance,
> with but a silent tear
> We dare not look behind us
> but steadfastly before
> We are coming, Father Abraham with
> three hundred thousand more
> We are coming, Father Abraham with
> three hundred thousand more."

More drum rolls followed the song, which was answered by the favorite song of the Confederacy, "Dixie." Jack lay back on the ground, praying that a snake wouldn't bite him and trying to decide what he should do. He couldn't move his foot that hurt so much. Mosquitoes buzzed around his head, sometimes biting him. His mother's tearful face and his father's stern admonishment to him about joining the Rebels brought tears to his eyes.

The sun bore down relentlessly during the day, and though the log gave him some protection from the heat, he was hot and thirsty. His clothes clung to him with sweat, and he longed to be cool and to drink some water. He wondered whether he had sustained any injuries from his fall into the ravine. His right ankle was hurting even worse, but he didn't know whether it might be sprained or possibly even broken. He didn't know what to do, other than continue to stay where he was. He tried to turn his head a little to look for his uncle's musket, but it had obviously fallen down between the logs in the abatis-choked ravine.

He longed for his uncle's water canteen back in the trench…oh! for a drink of water! As he tried to shift his position a little under the log, he looked through the peephole between leaves and branches and saw a solitary bluecoat, peering into the sap. The Yankee studied the ravine carefully, and Jack held his breath as the soldier took aim and fired. The bullet kicked up dirt and splinters from the logs and Jack closed his eyes to avoid their being hit by the debris. Obviously satisfied that no one was in the ravine, the soldier turned to leave as the Confederates sent a hail of bullets which knocked him over into the same ravine where Jack lay hidden.

"God in heaven, help me!" the soldier yelled as he floundered around among the logs and telegraph wire in the ravine. Jack lay as still as he could, knowing that he was in a scooped-out space under the log and below the sight of the soldier. After several minutes, when no sound came from the enemy soldier, Jack eased his head up to see what was going on.

He was sickened to see the soldier sitting against the side of the ditch with his legs sprawled out before him and blood oozing from his mouth and ears. His glazed eyes were fastened on the opposite wall of the ravine, and his musket must have fallen through the logs that filled the gully. Though Jack at first thought the soldier was dead, the Yankee moaned and tried to speak.

"Water…water…"

Jack grieved for the poor Yankee soldier, as he too was dying of thirst. Were they both to die together in the ravine for lack of water? As he lay back, trying to decide what to do, he heard a

Confederate officer in a connecting trench calling out to his men:

"Forward, my brave soldiers, and prepare to die!" At this, Jack could hear the fife and drum musicians render again the quick notes of "Dixie," and he heard his compatriots en masse negotiating the roughly hewn walls of the embankment to meet the enemy. He then heard the angry, shouted words from the oncoming federal army:

"Vicksburg or Hell!" was the rallying cry from the U. S. Army, and he could hear the terrible and angry shouts as men faced each other on the hilltops with their bullets and their bayonets, fighting hand to hand and killing one another.

Jack knew in his heart that this would probably be the final battle of the Vicksburg siege. He slightly raised his head to look at the Yankee soldier who still sat where he was before, but now his chin rested on his chest, with his mouth…and his eyes…closed. He appeared to be dead. However, Jack knew not to assume the soldier was dead. He had heard his father tell of Yankee soldiers shot dead by his father's unit, who played dead. They would appear to be dead, only to rebound when nudged by the enemy's boot.

As the afternoon wore on into beginning darkness, Jack lay in his tomb under the protecting log, afraid to move or to make any noise. He was certain he was dying as his thirst became unbearable. He prayed silently for water until he finally slipped into merciful sleep. The sounds of "Tattoo" from the bugles of the enemy, followed by "Taps" seeped into his consciousness.

"Hello?" Was he dreaming? It was totally dark now, he knew, but when he half-opened his eyes, he heard the screams and cries of the wounded and dying. Moonlight filtered softly into the ravine where he lay, and he could see the stars in the sky through the leaves and branches of the log which shielded him. Again, he heard a low sound.

"Jack?"

Jack opened his eyes and raised his head in the few inches of space between his face and the log above him. At first, he thought the wounded Yankee was calling his name, and being still half asleep, he wondered how a Yank would know his name. Again, he heard his name whispered, as a question.

"Jack?"

He was awake now and could see someone hurrying down the embankment which was across from him. When he reached the ravine, he began stepping over logs and telegraph wire, and he stopped to peer through the darkness at the Yankee who still sat with his head drooping to one side against the side of the ravine. In the moonlit darkness, Jack studied the form of the person calling his name and ventured a reply.

"I'm over here," he said through parched lips, attempting to extricate himself from the furrow under the log. Something about the man's voice was strangely familiar, and when he jumped over logs and debris to reach him, he suddenly revealed who he was.

"I'm here to help you, Jack," Stone Jackson said, as he removed the lid from his canteen and handed it to Jack. Jack was shaking as he reached for the water and drank profusely, until he finally quenched his thirst.

"Thank you, Stone," he said with tears in his eyes. "I thought I was going to die in this place! I've never been so thirsty in my life! How in the world did you find me?"

"I'll tell you all about it, Jack," Stone whispered, "but first I'm wondering about the Yankee over there," he said, nodding toward the soldier whose inert body lay near them. "Let me check and see if he's breathing."

"I've wondered about him, too," Jack said, feeling better now after drinking even more water.

Stone again stepped over logs and debris in the ravine to

reach the Yankee, first speaking in a low voice to him, then checking his wrist for a pulse. Shaking his head, he moved back over the logs and wire to Jack and whispered.

"He's gone. I was going to offer him water, but I'm afraid it's too late."

Stone joined Jack on the large log that had provided shelter during the recent battle, and Jack was first to whisper.

"Can you tell me how you happened to find me?"

"Well," Stone said in a low voice, "I had just returned from Jackson when the battle here was beginning, so I found a field glass and I looked over the ridges to the Confederate side. Actually, I had your Uncle Alan on my mind, yet what did I see but a young fellow with a gray slouch hat and a large red feather on the hat. Well, I knew it had to be you, Jack. Yes, I had gone to Jackson to carry a message from General Grant to General Sherman, but the real reason I agreed to go was to see whether I could help your father and brothers move to a safer place. From his last letter, your father mentioned that some of your cousins at Yellowsley's Crossing wanted them to spend the rest of the war with them. I found a wagon…couldn't find a carriage…and found another horse to help my horse pull the wagon there.

"Mr. Holmes was so glad to see me. He plied me with questions about you and Elise and your mother, also your aunt and uncle. He also wanted to write another letter to you all, so I have his letter with me. When it's daylight, you'll be able to read it."

Tears rolled down Jack's face as he reached over and hugged Stone' neck. Stone pulled the letter from his pants pocket and gave the letter to Jack who attempted to read it in the moonlight.

"There's just not enough light, Jack. I have a match, but it would bring unwanted attention to us here in the ravine. I didn't tell General Grant what I was going to do, so I don't know what

I'm in for, if he ever finds out," he said. Jack stuffed the letter into his shirt pocket. He thought about the fact that most of the Confederate uniforms didn't even have shirt pockets, but his mother had thoughtfully sewn one onto his uniform. And now it held a letter from his father! For the first time in weeks, he felt some happiness inside.

In a low voice, Stone said, "I've got to get you out of here some way. Can you walk?"

"I think so," Jack said, attempting to stand up. "Ow!" he muttered, when he tried to stand on his hurt foot.

"Seems like you hurt your foot," Stone said. "Do you think you can walk?"

"I'll try," Jack said. In excruciating pain, he attempted to step over the logs in the ravine, only to fall when his hurt foot gave way.

"We're going to have to get out of here before daylight, and we need to leave right now. I'm going to have to carry you out. Here," Stone said, "climb on my back."

"You can't carry me, Stone. I'll just…" Before Jack could finish protesting, Stone said, "I've had special training in carrying weight on my back. This is the only way you can get out of here. Climb on my back, little brother."

Jack reluctantly climbed onto Stone's back, remembering how he had recently come to think of Stone as the enemy, after seeing him at the Union fort with the northern General Grant.

"Let me find your musket," Stone said, looking for it and not finding it in the log-strewn ravine. "I don't see it, but I don't think you'll be needing it anymore. I believe this is the final battle for the city, so when daylight arrives, we should see the white flags of surrender appearing along the ridges. Hold on, little brother," Stone said as he stepped gingerly over tripping logs and wire in the ravine.

Stone began the difficult climb up the slanted but tremendous embankment with Jack holding on as well as he could. When they finally reached the ridge, Stone rested only a few seconds before crawling, face-first and with Jack still on his back, into the trench which Jack had left the day before.

The trek through the Confederate trench was a slow one, with Stone trying to find a pathway through the bodies of soldiers who had died from the battle and who lay where they had succumbed from enemy fire. Several times, soldiers who lay prostrate on the clay bottoms of the saps, but who were still alive, called out for water, and Stone gave them what was left in his canteen. Finally, they found themselves in the trench which led to the Confederate parapet, and after arriving at the parapet, Jack realized that Stone was wearing a Confederate uniform. Stone found a chair for Jack, and while they waited for an ambulance, Jack again thanked Stone profusely for helping him.

"Stone," Jack said, as he thought of his friend, Tommy, "My friend, Tommy Davis, was killed not many hours ago."

"Oh no! He was Elise's friend's brother, right?"

"That's right. He was like me...wanted to fight, but he got his head blown away...died in the sap we were digging."

"I'm so sorry, Jack. I'm thankful that you survived."

"Big brother," Jack said with tears in his eyes, "I think you may have saved my life and I thank you for it." It was the first time Jack had ever called Stone "big brother," and Stone reacted with a chuckle and grin.

"I don't know about that, little brother," he said, "but I remember hearing that your mother was surely upset when she saw you in your gray uniform. Of course, she never knew that you were actually going to fight. I think that would have killed her. She thought you were just going to carry messages for General Pemberton. She'll be thankful to see her young son again, especially when she realizes you were in the thick of battle. She'll be proud of you, little brother, now that you have come out of the battle alive, and I'm proud of you, too," Stone said, holding out his hand for Jack to shake it.

Jack grasped his hand and replied, "Thank you, big brother!" Jack held onto the chair where he sat and stood up, thankful to be alive, and though he winced with pain, he again threw his arms around Stone's neck, just as the ambulance arrived. Stone grinned at this and helped Jack into the ambulance.

In the light of early dawn, Jack told Stone goodbye as he was about to reenter the Confederate saps to return to the Union fort. When Stone was gone from his sight, Jack removed his father's folded letter from his pocket and read it. He was unaware that his tears wet the one-page letter which had no envelope. It was obviously written in haste.

"Dear loved ones, Abby, Elise, Jack, Alan, and Celia,

The boys and I are well. We are at our cousins' place at Yellowsley's Crossing, glad to be away from the chaos in Jackson. Jackson has been captured several times, and the flag over the courthouse has been taken down and repositioned to reflect which army has prevailed for the present time. The U. S. flag now flies over the courthouse, much to the anger of all of us Jacksonians. Our capital city is burned to the ground. Some call it "Chimneyville," since most of what's left are the chimneys. We miss all of you so much. I don't know what we would have done without Stone Jackson. He has offered to take my letter back to you. He secured a wagon and another horse which, along with his horse, managed to carry us and many of our valuables to our cousins' place at Yellowsley's Crossing. Maybe we will have some peace here. Please thank Mr. Jackson again for being so kind and helpful to me and to all of our family. We are all praying this war will be over soon, when we will be reunited.

Our love to all,
Wade and Mark and Jeremy"

Jack restored the letter to his pocket and asked the ambulance driver if he would take him first to the Holmes' cave, before going to a hospital. The driver obliged by directing the horses pulling the ambulance to the northern part of town, to the Holmes' cave. When they reached the cave, Elise was standing outside, having heard the horses and ambulance coming to the dugout. She looked shocked to see Jack arriving in the ambulance and was even more baffled and puzzled when the driver helped Jack, hopping on one foot, into the cave.

"Sir," Jack said to the driver, "Give me a few minutes with my sister, and I'll be ready to go to the hospital."

"I'll wait for you outside, young fellow," the driver said as he walked outside to the ambulance. Elise looked at Jack with a horrified and questioning look on her face.

"Jack, what has happened to you?" she asked.

"I was shot down and hurt my foot," Jack said. "You won't believe all I've been doing, Sis," Jack said, adding, "and you won't believe who saved my life." Elise stared at him, wanting him to hurry and tell her how he had been hurt and why he was on the way to the hospital.

"I saw you grab Uncle Alan's musket when you were here at the cave recently, but you didn't actually use it, did you?" she said.

"Yes, I did, Sister, and I nearly got myself killed. I took it with me into the saps which we were digging, and when we got orders to fight, well, I followed the other soldiers and climbed up the embankment with them. I couldn't load the musket quickly, and it was shot out of my hands, and I ended up in one of the ravines with logs and telegraph wire tripping me. I looked up and saw two Yanks reloading their muskets, so I slid under a big log to hide myself.

"Anyway, I knew my foot was hurt, but I didn't know how bad it was. I think it's badly sprained, but, Elise..." At this, Jack's eyes filled with tears. "Elise, while I was digging the trenches...you know, we couldn't stand up, because the saps weren't tall enough...anyway, Tommy Davis came in our sap and, Elise..., Tommy stood up and was killed by one of the Yankee sharpshooters." Elise screamed and caught herself with her hand over her mouth, remembering the ambulance driver waiting outside.

"Oh, Jack...oh no!" she whispered, her eyes filling with tears. "Oh, no! she said again. Recovering a little from the shock of it all, she thought to ask whether any of the Davis family knew what happened. "Oh, how terrible!" she cried.

"I don't know whether they have heard, or not. I'll let them know, if they haven't already heard. This was probably the last battle for the city, Elise, but I have to tell you who saved my life. I was so hot and thirsty in the ravine. I stayed under that log all day in the sun and I believe I would have died without water, when something miraculous happened." Elise could only stare at him, wanting him to finish what he was trying to say. She saw the tears that pooled in his eyes when he finally told her about being rescued.

"It was Stone...Stone Jackson who found me and gave me water. He said he'd know my hat with the red feather anywhere...said he looked through the field glass and was amazed to see me on the front lines. Oh, Sister," he said with tears rolling down his face, "he also brought us a letter from Papa." Jack withdrew the letter from his shirt pocket and handed it to Elise.

"I'll let you read it, then I'll take it to Mama, so she can read it, too," he said.

Elise was dumbfounded. Of the thousands of soldiers fighting, how could Stone have found her brother? She unfolded the letter and quickly read it, realizing all that Stone had gone through to move her father and her two younger brothers to safety. She wondered how he had managed to do it under the watchful eyes of Grant and possibly even the insufferable Sherman.

"Stone has kept us all alive, Jack," she said. Jack nodded mutely.

"I've never known anyone like him, Sis," Jack finally said.

"Nor I," Elise said.

Tears were in her eyes as she folded the letter and handed it back to Jack to give to their mother. Looking at his hurt foot, something told her that the heavy brogan on his foot should be removed before he returned to the ambulance. She felt certain that it was swollen, and she wondered whether the boot could even be removed. It would probably have to be cut off, if he waited any longer to take it off.

Jack, let me help you remove that boot on your hurt foot," she said. When he didn't protest, she knelt and untied the strings, trying to loosen them as much as possible, to give the foot more room for removal. Jack gritted his teeth as she carefully helped him to pull his foot from the brogan.

His foot was terribly swollen, as she had suspected. However, it didn't hang at an odd angle from his ankle. His foot might have some broken bones, but his ankle appeared to be all right. Maybe he had sprained his ankle. Whatever had happened, he needed to see a doctor.

The ambulance driver poked his head in the doorway of the cave just as the guns on the peninsula across from the city hammered a rapid-fire pounding on its buildings. This caused the driver to step quickly into the cave and the horses to rear up in fright.

"That's 100-pound Parrots!" he said in a voice of awe. "That's the worst volley yet! Our city is going to be reduced to rubble. It'll take us years to rebuild! Actually, I heard that General Pemberton is surrendering tomorrow, that there would be white flags appearing on the ridges tomorrow about this time, so I don't know what this heavy volley of Parrots means." As he ended speaking, suddenly there was a deathly silence over the city, followed by a strange medley of bugle calls along the Confederate parapet on the West and the trenches on the East. The city was surrendering.

"That's it!" the driver said. "That's the truce signal!" Elise and Jack stood still, not knowing what it meant.

"Young lady, you and your young brother here can be thankful that he wasn't hurt worse than he was, or even killed," the ambulance driver said. "I believe there's going to be a cease-fire pretty soon now," he added. They looked at one another, wondering what would happen next. and for the first time in months, since the siege began, no artillery was heard from the East or the West of the city.

"Yes… that was the truce signal," the driver said, adding, "I believe there's a cease-fire now, but there are a lot of bodies in the saps, I hear. I tell you, this is a sad day for Vicksburg and the South. We've gotten word that Lee failed at Gettysburg, so the war is pretty much over, I guess. Our soldiers put up a good fight, but we were outnumbered from the beginning. Grant had over 70,000 men, probably double what we had defending our city. And I guess we'll never know what happened to General Johnston. Yep, it's a sad, sad day for Vicksburg!"

"Thank you for letting me hear about the surrender tomorrow and also what the bugle blowing meant. I wouldn't have known, otherwise," Elise said.

"You're welcome, young lady," the driver said as Jack picked up his brogan and sock and, with the driver's and Elise's help, managed to hop back to the ambulance. The driver shook the reins over the horses' backs and Jack turned back and waved to Elise as the ambulance rolled on toward the hospital.

Elise sighed and went back into the cave. She wondered what would come next. Though she was all alone, she felt a certain happiness mingled with great relief, a feeling she had never experienced. For some reason, she couldn't feel the sadness that she probably should feel about the South possibly losing the war. All of her family were alive, miraculously, and she was alive. Somehow, they had managed to stay alive. And her father and brothers. They were faring better. This extraordinary and terrible time in the lives of all of them was coming to an end.

It was nearing the end of the brutal war, and the South was losing. Vicksburg had lost and it would take years to rebuild. Many homes and businesses were ruined, including her aunt's and uncle's home. Their plantation with its fields of cotton and its many slaves was gone. The slaves were gone forever, without a backward look.

For the first time, she began to see the structure of the southern economy. Her father had always told her that Mississippi produced more cotton than any other state, but the reason was that the cotton growers probably had more slaves to grow it and pick it. Now, with the invention of the cotton gin, they could grow even more, but…no…now there would be no slaves to harvest it.

Stone's words kept intruding on her thoughts as she sat in the cave, realizing the predicament and terrible dilemma he had found himself in when the war began. Her joy returned when she thought of Stone. Again, she wondered how in the world he had seen Jack and was able to rescue him. That big red feather on his hat was worth its weight in gold!

She suddenly looked around her, wondering what she was doing, sitting in the candle-lit, musty cave. Hadn't the ambulance driver told her there was a cease-fire now? She could leave the cave and never have to return to it.

"Oh, thank you, Lord above," she whispered as she left the dugout and began the uphill climb to the house. True to the words of the ambulance driver, there was no more firing now. In fact, an unearthly stillness and silence hovered over the city.

Elise hurried on up the embankment, immersed in her thoughts and thankful she would never have to live in a cave again. She planned to spend the night in the house, then go into town the next day. She wanted to bathe and put on a pretty dress…no more drab homespun! She never again wanted to see another dark, ugly homespun dress! She hurried into the house and stopped at the cistern to bathe and wash her hair. The water was cold, but oh…how wonderful not to have to worry about shells bombing the house or even killing her. She used her aunt's perfumed soap and enjoyed a luxurious bath with no one to hurry her and no Yanks to frighten her.

Chapter Ten

Elise stood in front of the open armoire, trying to decide which dress to wear. She wondered whether she would see Stone today. She knew without a doubt that she would see him soon. There was something in the Bible, she mused, about a woman adorning herself for her husband, and she intended to do just that. He wasn't her husband yet, but she could pretend that he was.

She closed the door of the large armoire and looked at herself in the beveled mirror on its door. Would her eyes ever lose their look of hunger and fear? She had lost so much weight. Her clothes would hang on her, as the homespun ones did now.

Well, I have to dress, she thought to herself. The war is over…thank God…, she continued with her musings. I'll go into town and see Mama and Jack and Aunt Celia and Uncle Alan…oh, thank you God! She said these things to herself with her hands clasped as in prayer and her eyes closed.

And Stone…oh, Lord, does he want to see me as much as I want to see him? Her thoughts tumbled about in her mind as she selected a summer dress of pastel flowers. It had a sash around the waist which would help to hide her thinness. She found her brush and began brushing her long hair. Next, she looked in her toilet table chest which she had brought with her from Jackson, something she hadn't done during the entire 47-day-long siege. She planned to look her prettiest for the man she loved, even if he was a reviled Yank, she sighed ruefully. After all, she and her family…and others in the nearby caves were alive because of him.

Finding rosewater in the small chest, she knew it had lost

its freshness, so she couldn't use it. She had last used it for the ball not long after arriving in Vicksburg. She did use some of the lavender dusting powder, however. Rubbing some blush on her lips, she looked at herself in the small mirror over the dressing table. She remembered the advice from her mother, when she became old enough to use makeup, that a little would enhance but too much would detract.

Now that she was ready to walk into town, she looked at herself again in the oval mirror on the door of the armoire. Again, she mused that she should feel some sorrow about Vicksburg being captured and about the South likely losing the war, especially since Gettysburg and now Vicksburg had fallen. She knew that her life and the lives of her family and indeed everyone in the South would be forever uprooted and changed. She wondered what the future held for all of them. However, she had some hope now, whereas for six weeks, she had none. The thought of not having to live in the cave another day and fight for survival every minute and not know whether she would have anything to eat from day to day made tears of appreciation come to her eyes.

As she was about to leave the room, she heard the catchy notes of "Dixie" coming from the music room below. She held her breath, wondering who was in the house and who was playing the piano. When she started down the stairway, she heard the conclusion of the southern song, which was followed by a brief pause and then the majestic notes of "The Battle Hymn of the Republic."

She knew without a doubt who was seated at the piano. She wondered whether there was anything Stone Jackson could not do. She knew he was also playing by ear, as she had looked for the music to both of the songs and had not found it. She had studied about the Renaissance at the academies she had attended, and she learned a term which applied to Stone Jackson. He was a

"Renaissance man." And he loved her, Celia Elise Holmes!

As she listened to the powerful rendition of the music, a sense of joy and peace flooded over her. It was an antidote to the terror and hopelessness of the past two months. She stood in the parlor, waiting for Stone to finish playing the song which the Union army had taken as its own.

When Stone played the last note, he closed the lid on the piano before standing up and walking into the parlor. He held out his arms and Elise fled to him. She threw her arms around his neck and he held her, kissing her face and neck and mouth.

"Are you ready to marry me, Elise?" he asked softly.

"I think I've been ready since I first met you, Stone," she said.

"Maybe we can get the Reverend Lord to perform the ceremony. How about that?"

"Sounds great to me," Elise said.

"I've got something to show you," Stone said, picking up several issues of the local newspaper *The Daily Citizen* which he had laid on a table in the parlor.

"I had heard they were printing on the back of wallpaper," he said with a chuckle. "Some ingenuity," he added. "Yes, we would read some of those issues in the cave," Elise said.

"Well, this is the July 2nd issue. Have you seen it?"

"No, let me see it."

When Stone handed her the paper, he pointed to a short article on the front page. Elise read it out loud:

"On Dit. That the great Ulysses—the Yankee Generalissimo, surnamed Grant—has expressed his intention of dining in Vicksburg on Saturday next, and celebrating the 4th of July by a grand dinner and so forth. When asked if he would invite Gen. Jo. Johnston to join him, he said 'No! For fear there will be a row at the table.' Ulysses must get into the city before he dines in it. The way to cook a rabbit is 'first catch the rabbit' &c."

Elise smiled after reading the article, and Stone handed her the day-later issue of the same newspaper. "Well," he said, "when the Union army finally entered the city, they found the type still standing and decided to issue the paper again with the addition of the following note. Now, read this July 4th edition," he said, handing her the paper. Elise read this article aloud, also:

"Two days bring about great changes; the banner of the Union floats over Vicksburg. Gen. Grant has 'caught the rabbit,' he has dined in Vicksburg, and he did bring his dinner with him. *The Citizen* lives to see it. For the last time it appears on 'Wallpaper.' No more will it eulogize the luxury of mule meat and fricasseed kitten, urge Southern warriors to such diet never more. This is the last wallpaper edition, and is, excepting this note, from the types as we found them. It will be valuable hereafter as a curiosity."

"I'm just thankful it's over, Stone," Elise said, shaking her head and smiling. "Little did I realize when we left Jackson on the train just a little over two months ago that we were literally jumping out of the frying pan into the fire, as my mother would say."

"Well, I would never have met you, if you hadn't come," Stone said, kissing her on her upturned mouth. "Now," he said, "I've got to see about Blackberry…remember him?" Stone said, as they both looked out the parlor window at the large horse.

"I've got some things I want to show you in your aunt's backyard, also," he said, opening the front door for her. As they walked toward the driveway, the horse whinnied and pawed the dirt in recognition. When Stone freed him from being tethered to the low-lying limb of a nearby tree, he led him over to Elise who reached up and stroked the horse's neck.

Holding Stone's hand, Elise walked with him and

Blackberry to her aunt's backyard where Stone led the horse to the nearest stream for water and also surrounding grass to graze. Though he secured the horse again, he gave him the freedom to move about and nibble at the grass while he and Elise walked about the shell-riven acreage. When they approached another stream where Elise remembered seeing the beaver family, she noticed that the dam was larger but she didn't see the beavers.

"Guess they're resting from their labors," Stone said with a laugh. He then led her to the large mulberry tree where she had seen blue eggs several weeks before. Now, when they looked into the nest, they saw four baby birds with their feathers intact and their mouths open. Shards of their blue shells were scattered about the nest, remnants from their incubation only a few weeks before. As Elise was wondering where the mother bird was, she heard the almost musical "chur-lee, chur-lee" from the branches above and was surprised to see two bluebirds, one doing the chirping and the other with a caterpillar in its mouth. She was likely the mother. Was the vocal one the father? she wondered.

On their walk back to the front driveway, their shoes crunched on the spent shells lying all over the yard. They both glanced at the huge missile which left the large hole in the side of her aunt's house. Stone's repair efforts with wood from the rail fence seemed to be holding up. Elise knew that her aunt and uncle would stay busy a long time, making repairs to their lovely home. She wondered how in the world they could produce cotton now, or any crop, without slaves to plant it and tend it and harvest it.

Stone took Elise's hand and they began the walk to the downtown area of Vicksburg. It was a beautiful but hot day in early July. The sky was so blue that Stone compared it to the blue of Elise's eyes. She was certain that her eyes were not that beautiful shade of blue, but it pleased her for Stone to say such a thing. Also, she knew she shouldn't have such joy in her heart, but it was there, waiting to burst forth when she didn't have to hide it before the citizenry and the soldiers who had fought so long and so hard to protect the city and to win the battle. She knew that Stone had convinced her that the states in their country were better united than fragmented, and that's what the terrible war was finally settling.

The blue hues of far-off hills across the river and the distant Louisiana woods lent a certain serenity to a quiet summer day. Other than birds chirping, the silence was almost deafening, considering that she and the rest of the populace of Vicksburg had been subjected to continuous cannonading of artillery every minute of every day for the past several weeks or longer. She was having to readjust her thinking. No longer was she having to dodge bullets and wonder whether she would be living the next minute of every day.

As they approached the downtown area, they could see Federal soldiers breaking open stores and plundering them. Vicksburg merchants who had hoarded supplies during the siege began selling their wares for outlandish prices. Flour was selling for $400 a barrel, sugar for $30 a barrel, and coffee for $10 a pound. Other merchants were selling wines which the citizens of the city had craved in vain during the siege. A lot of food had been withheld by the Confederate government, and this was rolled out into the streets by early arrivals of the conquering Union army.

"Here Rebs, help yourselves; you are naked and starving and need them!" they yelled.

The emaciated troops grabbed what they could and began eating what they could, at the same time stacking their arms and cartridge boxes and flags at a designated place, according to orders they had received from the Union generals. The difference between the well-fed Union army and the thin, vermin-infested Confederate soldiers, along with the townspeople, was heart-rending to Elise.

Suddenly, it appeared that all eyes were on the courthouse

which had taken so much mistreatment by the shells of the enemy during the battle. A large crowd of blue-clad Union soldiers were watching as one of their own climbed up the façade of the building and retrieved the flag of the 45th Illinois regiment which had first replaced the stars and bars of the Confederate flag, at General Grant's instigation. This flag was duly folded in solemn ceremony and given to an officer from the hometown of the regiment. All of this, Stone explained to Elise as they watched the ceremony.

After this, another Union soldier, holding the large United States flag, began the climb to the cupola of the courthouse. After reaching the flag receptacle, he affixed the standard and as he began the descent to the ground, a breeze opened the flag which billowed in its full glory, its thirty-four stars evident to all who watched below. The blue horde of soldiers watching below first clapped, then began singing the "Battle Hymn of the Republic."

As their strong voices sounded over the town, a woman standing near Elise and Stone began ranting and shouting. "The murderous Yankees may celebrate today, but I never will!" she screamed, adding, "Never again!" Others nearby voiced their opinions and displeasure, also. Some openly accused General Pemberton for the surrender of the city, but many blamed General Johnston for not coming to their aid. Elise's heart ached for them. Would the people of the South ever become a part of the United States again? Would she ever feel the same toward her country, she wondered?

Hearing the enraged and bitter voices of many of their own soldiers nearby, Elise saw members of the Third Louisiana Infantry cursing and yelling as they broke their rifles against trees and scattered ammunition over the ground. Then, they tore their battle-worn flags into shreds.

As Elise and Stone stood there, witnessing the sorrow of

the surrendering city, a corporal who said his name was Abner J. Wilkes of the 46th Regiment of the Mississippi Infantry voiced his opinion so that all could hear:

"We were there just 48 days and nights, penned up like so many hogs in a pen," he said. "We never could have been wiped out there but General Pemberton sold us to the Yankees at some price. But I can say we gave them Hail Columbia for 48 days and nights!" After hearing this, someone nearby volunteered that Pemberton was seen crawling out of a cave only the day before. Elise wondered whether this was actually true.

The citizens of Vicksburg swarmed out of their caves and cellars, thankful that the long ordeal was finally over. They gathered in the sunshine in the main streets of downtown Vicksburg. They had heard that there were provisions on the Union boats…flour and coffee… which were preparing to come down the river in a full display of victory and glory. While some of the starving populace waited at the river's edge for the gunboats, others who were able roamed through the streets with their arms full of canned goods.

Stone commented on the crudely built skiffs that were piled near the river, and Elise told him that Jack had told all of them in their cave about them. She told him that Jack's hands were torn and bleeding from pulling wood from houses to build the boats, as General Pemberton had requested. She commented that she would have been fearful to trust the hurriedly built boats to ferry them across the river. Stone was amazed that such was going on during the time he had been away. He was unaware that boats were being built to convey the populace across the river.

One of the Federal officers walked over to them as they stood watching the massive display of victory and surrender which was being acted out before them. The officer saluted Stone at which time Stone introduced him to Elise. At Stone's request, the officer told them the condition of the Confederate holdout.

"Well, it seems we have 31,600 prisoners, together with 172 cannons, about 60,000 muskets and a large amount of ammunition," he said. "Also," he added, "General Grant wants the trenches filled...that'll take several months, if not longer, and I believe he's going to grant all of the prisoners parole."

"Yes, I had heard as much, also," Stone said, adding, "We want the prisoners to be well treated."

"Yes, Sir!" the officer said with another salute as he turned and walked away.

As Elise and Stone walked toward the Old Landing, where so many of the citizens of the town were gathering at the river, someone shouted, "They're coming! They're coming!" Elise felt chills going over her body, even in the hot July sun, as she looked up the river and saw the vast Federal fleet heading toward the river landing. Gunboat after gunboat, transport after transport, broadside after broadside with colorful signal flags flying and bands playing heralded the pure joy of a victory dearly won. Streamers and pennons fluttered, along with blaring music and blowing whistles. The transports were trimmed with bunting and United States flags and were filled with smartly dressed Union soldiers in their best uniforms, presumably saved for just this special occasion.

Hearing the march of tramping boots behind them, Elise and Stone looked back and saw the blue multitude of the Union army bearing down upon them, with General Ulysses Grant astride his horse, leading the way. As they marched, they shouted as one:

"Hip, hip, hurrah! Hip, hip, hurrah!" Elise marveled at the stalwart, well-fed men on their sleek, U. S. horses in comparison to the suffering men in gray, who were still stacking their weapons in the assigned area of the town.

"The army of the occupation is coming!" someone yelled, and Elise wondered whether there would be jeers and insults from the conquering army toward the vanquished men who stared at their captors as they marched abreast, in columns, toward them. As they drew nearer, wearing shiny white paper collars and white gloves and marching in strict military formation, with their generals riding their glossy horses and with well-polished arms and bright plumes displaying the magnificent panoply and pride of the victorious army, a hearty cheer was rendered by one of the Federal divisions for the "gallant warriors of Vicksburg!"

Marching in beat, in front of the massive columns of thousands of Union soldiers, the drum and fife corps suddenly brought their musical instruments to life with a rendition of "Hail Columbia," causing tears to come to the eyes of many of the Yankee soldiers. Some of the soldiers in front began singing the words to the song, and all along the columns of the victorious army, their voices swelled in sheer joy and harmony.

There was little or no arrogance and no insults from the conquering army. In fact, once the soldiers mixed and mingled with the Confederates and the citizenry near the river, the Yankee soldiers began sharing what food they had managed to bring with them to the starving Rebels. However, everyone moved to the sides of the street to allow General Grant and his top officers to meet the transports on the river which were waiting at the landing for them.

Every vessel of the navy sounded its whistle in celebration as General Grant dismounted and boarded Porter's flagship, the USS Benton, to shake the hand of the navy Commander whose fleet had provided backup support during the entire lengthy battle. The brass of their medals and insignias sparkled in the summer sun when several shots were fired, making Elise jump, as both leaders grasped hands in victory, their faces wreathed in smiles.

"Those were blank shots, Elise, honey, not real ones," Stone said, putting his arm around her and drawing her to him.

As the Federal army continued to dole out food to the

starving Rebel soldiers, Elise heard a woman weeping as though her heart would break. Turning around, she saw Sybil Adams, clutching her newborn baby while Carrie and Adeline clung to her.

"Oh, Miss Elise," she cried. "I need someone to help me. Oh, God in heaven, help me!" she sobbed, bowing her head, then looking up into the sky.

Before Elise could answer her, Stone took her by the hand and they hurried over to the distraught mother. Carrie and Adeline ran to Elise and hugged her, prompting Elise to pick up the smaller child and introduce both of them to Stone.

"These were my cave neighbors," she said, introducing the girls first, then putting Adeline down, she introduced their mother to Stone.

"Glad to meet you, Mrs. Adams," he said. "Is there some way we can help you?"

"It's my baby," Sybil Adams said with tears still streaming from her eyes.

"Oh, let me see little Vick," Elise said, looking at the baby which was wrapped in a small towel. Elise was shocked at the baby's appearance. Though he was crying with his little face contorted and his eyes closed, he was making such a low, mewing sound that no one could hear him with all of the noise around them.

"I don't have enough milk for my baby," Sybil Adams said, not caring that she spoke of such intimate matters in the presence of a man she did not know. Elise knew her former neighbor was desperate.

"I paid a young boy to milk a cow for Victor, so I'd have enough milk for him," she said, "but some of our own soldiers came and got the cow. I begged them not to do it, but they wouldn't listen to me. Oh, Miss Elise, my baby is starving! Please, can either of you help me?"

"I can help you, Mrs. Adams," Stone said. "Just follow

Elise and me to the officer over there," he said, reaching down and picking up both of the little girls who sensed that he was going to help their mother in her dire situation.

"Elise, you and Mrs. Davis, follow me. We're going to see about this right now."

When the blue-coated officer saw them coming toward him, he moved toward them with a smile and a salute to Stone. Stone put the girls down and returned the salute.

"Officer Bowen, Mrs. Adams needs some assistance now, as of this minute. The cow which was supplying her baby's milk was stolen and her baby needs to be fed as quickly as possible."

"I'll see to it!" the officer said, clicking his heels and saluting before turning to Sybil Adams. "Please follow me, Mrs. Adams," he said.

"Oh, thank you, sir...thank you!" Sybil Adams exclaimed, gathering her two girls. Turning to Elise and Stone, she thanked them fervently before speaking alone to Elise.

"Miss Elise," she said hurriedly, "you have helped me so much during this entire ordeal. When things settle down and get back to normal, and I hope it won't be too long, I want to do something special for you. I love you, Miss Elise."

Her heartfelt words brought tears to Elise's eyes. "I love you and your children, also," she said.

As they left with the officer, Stone put his arm around Elise and asked her a question that brought joy to her heart.

"Do you think Reverend Lord would perform our marriage ceremony today?" he asked.

"I don't know, but we can find out," Elise said, going along with his banter.

"I'm serious," he said, looking earnestly into her eyes.

"Well, we will have to find him," Elise said. "I've heard that the rectory is in bad shape from all of the bombing, and the

Lords moved into one of the caves. We'll have to find him. Too, I am wondering whether Jack has been able to talk to Drusie and her family about Tommy. I know they must be devastated. If Uncle Alan hadn't been in the hospital, he could have prevented it. But then, I think about Jack. Uncle Alan could have prevented his going into the battle, too. I wonder how badly his foot was hurt. I want to see my mother and Jack and my Aunt Celia and Uncle Alan, also Drusie and her parents. Maybe they will all be well enough to attend our wedding," she said. "I only wish that Papa and Mark and Jeremy could be here, also," she added.

"I, too, wish they could be here and also my family," Stone said with a smile as they began the walk back to the caves in search of the pastor. "Yes, I also heard that the rectory took a beating due to direct missile hits, but maybe we can find the good rector. I want you to meet my brothers and my parents, also, Elise. I think they will like the fact that I married a true Southern lady."

Irrepressible joy welled in Elise's heart as she slipped her hand into Stone's. She glanced at the United States flag that now billowed over the city of Vicksburg, its thirty-four stars reflecting the unity of all of the states. Yes, Elise thought, one of those stars symbolizes the State of Mississippi which, like an errant child, had gone astray and was now back in the fold of the Union.

Elise At Vicksburg

Battle of Vicksburg Pictures

Fig 1.

LIEUTENANT-GENERAL J. C. PEMBERTON, C. S. A.
FROM A PHOTOGRAPH.

Fig. 2

VICKSBURG COURT HOUSE, A LANDMARK DURING THE SIEGE. FROM A PHOTOGRAPH TAKEN IN 1880.

Fig. 3

COLONEL S. H. LOCKETT, C. S. A.,
CHIEF ENGINEER OF THE VICKSBURG DEFENSES.
FROM AN OIL PORTRAIT.

Fig. 4

PASSAGE, ON THE NIGHT OF APRIL 16, 1863, OF GUN-BOATS AND STEAMERS AT VICKSBURG. FROM A SKETCH MADE BY COLONEL S. H. LOCKETT, C. S. A.

Fig. 5

REAR-ADMIRAL PORTER'S FLOTILLA PASSING THE VICKSBURG BATTERIES, NIGHT OF APRIL 16, 1863, THE FLAG-SHIP "BENTON" LEADING, FOLLOWED BY THE "LOUISVILLE," "LAFAYETTE," "GENERAL PRICE," "MOUND CITY," "PITTSBURG," "CARONDELET," AND "TUSCUMBIA"; AND THE TRANSPORTS "HENRY CLAY," "FOREST QUEEN," AND "SILVER WAVE." FROM A WAR-TIME SKETCH.

Fig. 6

REAR-ADMIRAL PORTER'S FLOTILLA ARRIVING BELOW VICKSBURG ON THE NIGHT OF APRIL 16, 1863 — IN THE FOREGROUND GENERAL W. T. SHERMAN GOING IN A YAWL TO THE FLAG-SHIP "BENTON."

Fig.7

GENERAL BLAIR'S DIVISION CROSSING BIG BLACK RIVER. FROM A WATER-COLOR.

Fig. 8

WOODEN COEHORN ON GRANT'S LINES. FROM A SKETCH MADE AT THE TIME.

Fig. 9

THE FIGHT IN THE CRATER AFTER THE EXPLOSION OF THE UNION MINE UNDER THE CONFEDERATE FORT ON THE JACKSON ROAD, JUNE 25, 1863. FROM A LITHOGRAPH.

To the right and left are seen part of the approaches from the main Union line at the White House, as shown in the plan on p. 540.

Fig. 10

GENERAL GRANT.   MASTER FRED. D. GRANT.   CHARLES A. DANA, ASSISTANT SECRETARY OF WAR.

UNION HEADQUARTERS, JULY 3. GENERAL GRANT RECEIVING GENERAL PEMBERTON'S MESSAGE. FROM A SKETCH MADE AT THE TIME.

Works Cited

Fig.1. Lieutenant-General J.C. Pemberton, C.S.A. *Battles and Leaders of the Civil War* (p. 474), by Union and Confederate Officers, New York: Thomas Yoseloff, Inc. 1956.

Fig.2. Vicksburg Court House. *Battles and Leaders of the Civil War* (p. 480), by Union and Confederate Officers, New York: Thomas Yoseloff, Inc. 1956.

Fig.3. Colonel S. H. Lockett, C.S.A. *Battles and Leaders of the Civil War* (p. 481), by Union and Confederate Officers, New York: Thomas Yoseloff, Inc. 1956.

Fig.4. Passage, on the night of April 16, 1863. *Battles and Leaders of the Civil War* (p. 485), by Union and Confederate Officers, New York: Thomas Yoseloff, Inc. 1956.

Fig.5. Bear-Admiral Porter's Flotilla. *Battles and Leaders of the Civil War* (p. 496), by Union and Confederate Officers, New York: Thomas Yoseloff, Inc. 1956.

Fig.6. Bear-Admiral Porter's Flotilla Below Vicksburg. *Battles and Leaders of the Civil War* (p. 497), by Union and Confederate Officers, New York: Thomas Yoseloff, Inc. 1956.

Fig.7. General Blair's Division. *Battles and Leaders of the Civil War* (p. 514), by Union and Confederate Officers, New York: Thomas Yoseloff, Inc. 1956.

Fig.8. Wooden Coehorn on Grant's Lines. *Battles and Leaders of the Civil War* (p. 522), by Union and Confederate Officers, New York: Thomas Yoseloff, Inc. 1956.

Fig.9. The Fight in the Crater. *Battles and Leaders of the Civil War* (p. 527), by Union and Confederate Officers, New York: Thomas Yoseloff, Inc. 1956.

Fig.10. Union Headquarters. *Battles and Leaders of the Civil War* (p. 532), by Union and Confederate Officers, New York: Thomas Yoseloff, Inc. 1956.